Our Love Is
A
Life
Sentence

Rae Zellous

Our Love Is A Life Sentence

Our Love Is A Life Sentence

Copyright © 2017 by Rae Zellous

All rights reserved. No part of this publication may be reproduced, distributed, or transmitted in any form or by any means, including photocopying, recording, or other electronic or mechanical methods, without the prior written permission of the publisher, except in the case of brief quotations embodied in critical reviews and certain other noncommercial uses permitted by copyright law.

Cover Art by Graphic Designer

Edited by So Amazing Literary Services

Our Love Is A Life Sentence

ACKNOWLEDGMENTS

CHAPTER 1

THE DAY OF SENTENCING, Devanna "Diva" British, got her crying, three-year-old son, Baby Roman, dressed. "Ssshhh, put'cha hand in," she said to him, putting his arm through the ride side of his Marvel Comics t-shirt. It had the picture of the Black Panther on it. Diva tried to hush him as she dressed him. She let him sleep while she showered, and got dressed. Now he was fussing because she had woken him up.

"Come on, baby. I know...I know," she said as he cried. She was a good mother, and very patient when it came to her son. She was on her way to the Federal Courthouse Downtown Pittsburgh. Her son's father, "Roman Edmonds Sr.," was being sentenced. It had been almost two years since his arrest, and being a single parent had become a struggle for her more and more each day. She wasn't struggling financially, but emotionally. After putting on Baby Roman's hoodie, she gave him his bottle, and called his grandmother, Marielle Edmonds, "Ma, I'm on my way ... Okay," she said, leaving out of her front door.

It was eighty degrees in Pittsburgh on the twenty-seventh day of July. The heat was stifling. Diva sat at a traffic light a couple minutes away from the federal building. Pedestrians walked the city streets in singular and pairs. Some drinking bottled water, placing the chilled plastic to their foreheads trying to keep cool. Others fanned themselves and wiped sweat from their foreheads standing at the T-Station, where people stood to catch their buses. Diva was trying to figure out where she was going to park, "Ma, should I park where we did last time?" She asked her boyfriend's mother. They had been to the courthouse in support of Roman several times during his two years stay in prison. This would be the last court appearance unless he found grounds to appeal.

"Girl, I don't know," Roman's mother, Marielle, responded as she massaged her eyes with her fingers. She had been up all night worrying about her son. He was her only son, and she planned on telling the judge how much he meant to her... In attempts to get him lesser time. Roman was looking at twenty years, but the government was offering a deal of ten years and eight years of probation.

"Nah, I'll just park in the parking garage by the Greyhound Bus Station. That way I won't have to worry about getting towed," Diva said. The parking garage was across from the courthouse. She knew exactly where she was going to park. She was just trying to make small talk. This process had been hard on both but on this sunny day stress was setting in Marielle's face and she began to worry about her.

"That sounds about right. I know you don't want that to happen. You already have enough going on in ya life," Marielle said, rolling her eyes, and grunting at the thought. With a slight grin on her face.

INSIDE A HOLDING CELL at the Federal Courthouse, "Edmonds, ya lawyer wants to see you," a US Marshall said to Roman. Roman got up from resting on the stainless-steel bench inside of the holding cell. Once he stepped out of the cell the Marshall placed him in handcuffs and walked him around to the interviewing rooms. They were located on the other side of the holding cells.

The Marshall unlocked the door of the interviewing room number one, where Roman's lawyer, Samuel Sholar awaited. Roman stepped inside, and the Marshall removed his handcuffs. After he took a seat on the steel stool in the room the Marshall stepped out of the interviewing room and closed the steel door. The heavy weight of the steel door slammed into its frame behind him, and the sound of the door locking echoed throughout the empty hallway.

"How you feelin'?" Samuel Sholar asked his client through a steel screen divider.

"I'm aight. It is what it is, you know?" Roman said, looking at his lawyer sideways.

"Well Roman, you could have been on your way home with time served if you would have cooperated."

"And I tol'cha ass I would've done twenty if I had to. I'm not testifying on my niggas!"

8

Our Love Is A Life Sentence

"You know what I don't understand?" The attorney asked.
"What? What don't you understand, Sam!"
"I don't understand how you are whim' to do twenty years for a group of individuals that don't give a fuck about you. Are they more important than your mother, your girlfriend or your son?"
"Fuck no! But see you'll never understand the street code 'cause ya not from the streets! Roman told his lawyer.
 "Now you wanna know what I don't understand?" Roman asked his lawyer.
"What's that?"
"How did I pay you over eighty stacks, and I'm still pleading to the fucking guidelines," Roman continued.
"I put my career on the line for you, Roman! understand that! Besides, I told you from the start the only way around the mandatory minimum is to cooperate," the attorney reminded his client. What upset him, and wasn't explained in detail was attorney Sam Sholar had a bad gambling habit that almost cost him his firm. Confiding in Roman, Roman made him a proposition, and soon after Samuel Sholar began to bring drugs into the prison system for his client.

"Shit! We both benefited. You talk about losing ya career, I saved it!" Roman reminded his lawyer, with his eyebrows bunched and lip curled.

"Look, Roman, I did everything in my power to get you under the mandatory minimum. This is the best offer the government is offering. We can go to trial if that's what you want?"

"Whateva! Let's just get this shit over with," Roman said, shifting in his seat.

Samuel Sholar looked at Roman quietly for a few seconds, "Okay, they will be calling you upstairs, shortly."

"Is my mom and my girl up there?" Roman asked.

"Yes, they are, but ya homies aren't."

"Man, whateva!"

"I'll tell the Marshall we're done."

IN THE COURTROOM Roman looked behind him to get a glance at his mother and his girl as the District Attorney spoke to the court, "On September 16, 2011, the grand jury returned a three-count indictment against Edmonds and eight other individuals. Edmonds was charged with Count One with conspiracy to distribute one kilogram or more of heroin in violation of 21 U.S.C 846. The government filed a notice pursuant to 21 U.S.C §851 on March 11 of this year, 2013. The filing of this motion subjected Edmonds to an enhanced mandatory minimum sentence of twenty years imprisonment upon conviction. Edmonds proceeded to trial on May 5, 20131 On May 7, 2013, Edmonds entered a plea of guilty in accordance with a written plea agreement.

Under the terms of the plea agreement, Edmonds agreed to plead guilty to a lesser-included offense: conspiracy to distribute 100 grams or more of heroin. This provision of the agreement reduced the applicable mandatory minimum term of imprisonment from twenty to ten years. The parties also, agreed that a term of incarceration of 120 months of imprisonment would be an appropriate sentence in Edmonds' case," District Attorney Mary Goldberg stated to the Court. Explaining that Roman pleaded guilty during the midst of trial, the government's section 851 notice was filed prior to trial. If Roman had been convicted of the charged offense, he would have been subjected to a minimum sentence of twenty years.

"Mr. Edmonds, is this true? Do you wish to change the plea you previously entered at Count 1 of the indictment to a plea of guilty and let me just look over this plea for a second?" the judge, Ellis Reeves, said, taking a few minutes to examine the document that was before him.

"Alright, you are also pleading to a lesser included offense, you are pleading guilty to conspiracy to distribute and possess with intent to distribute 100 grams or more of heroin, is this right, Mr. Edmonds?"

"Yes, your Honor.

"Before accepting your guilty plea, there are a number of questions that I'ma ask you to make certain your plea is valid. If you do not understand any question, please let me know and I will explain it to you. If at any time you need to speak with your lawyer, Mr. Sholar, let me know that and I will give you as much time as you need to speak to him. I am giving you these instructions because it is very important that you understand every question before you answer."

After a series of questions the judge made note that Roman's maximum penalty, if he were convicted, would have been a term of imprisonment not less than ten years and up to life in prison; a fine of $4 million; a term of supervised release of not less than eight years, and an assessment of $100 1ursuant to federal law, the District Attorney spoke again, "Your honor Mr. Edmonds understands that the United States Attorney has already filed an information pursuant to Title 21, United States Code, Section 851, stating one prior conviction as a basis for increased punishment."

Roman looked back at Diva and his mother, and mouthed the words, "That's some bullshit," without actually saying a word. Then the District Attorney began to explain to the Court exactly what Roman and his co-defendant were guilty, summarizing the government's evidence, "The investigation, in this case, culminated in wiretaps on at least a dozen cell phones utilized by Edmonds and several others. Mr. Edmonds was linked to York/New Jersey area. Among other things, wiretaps, December 2010, through mid-September and heroin connection in the New which was conducted from the end 2011, revealed that Mr. Edmonds helped arrange, broker, and helped facilitate large heroin transactions equaling up to the amount of one kilogram of heroin between heroin suppliers in the New York/New Jersey area and street-level drug dealers in Pittsburgh Pennsylvania Based on this evidence, the government would prove at trial and at sentencing that during the charged time frame, Mr. Edmonds conspired with others, both known and unknown, to distribute and possess with intent to distribute heroin, and the amount of heroin personally attributable to Mr. Edmonds is at least 100 grams but no less than 400 grams," hearing the evidence made Diva's eyes water. She had heard it before during trial, but then it was arguable. This was sentencing, and her man was agreeing to have sold the amount the DA was speaking about.

Meaning she knew her man was going away for a very long time. Roman's mother put her arm around her shoulders and pulled her into her breast, "He'll be aight, baby. God got 'im," Marielle told Diva, consoling her in a low whisper.

"You heard the evidence, did you not, Mr. Edmonds?" The Judge asked Roman.

"Yes, ya Honor, I did," Roman said.

"Do you agree with what he said accurately describes what you did?"

"Yes, ya Honor."

"Mr. Sholar, is it your advice that Mr. Edmonds plead guilty?"

"Yes, your Honor,"! Roman's lawyer said.

Mr. Edmonds, because you acknowledge you are, in fact, guilty as charged in a lesser included offense to Count 1 of the indictment, because you know about your right to trial, because you know the maximum penalty that could be imposed if you are convicted of this offense after trial and because you are voluntarily pleading guilty, I will accept your guilty plea and enter a judgement of guilty on your plea to a lesser included offense of Count 1 of the Indictment at No. 12-020.

It is the finding of the Court in the case of the United States of America against Roman Edmonds, Mr. Edmonds is fully competent and capable of entering an informed plea, his plea of guilty is knowing and voluntary and supported by an independent basis, in fact, containing each of the essential elements of the offense.

Therefore, the plea is accepted and the defendant Roman Edmonds is now adjudged guilty of a lesser included offense of the charge contained in Count 1 of the indictment..."

"Ah-ah-ah-ah," Diva cried out. Roman looked back at her. The sight of his woman being held by his teary-eyed mother made him weak. He quickly turned back towards the judge as she continued. "...Mr. Edmonds and counsel, please sign the change of plea," the judge said, removing her glasses from her face. She was a senior judge in her sixties or so.

Roman and his lawyer signed the plea agreement, "Your Honor my client requested that his sentencing is expedited. I believe you have the motion I filed there. Myself and the District Attorney spoke about this and he doesn't have a problem if you don't. Ah, my client would like to be transferred from federal holding as soon as possible. As you see..." Roman's lawyer pointed at Diva and his mother. "...Another court hearing would be too heartbreaking for his family," Samuel Sholar said.

"Mrs. Goldberg to you have any objections?"

"No, your honor. I'm also ready to get this case behind me."

"Okay then, let's get on with it. Is there anyone here that would like to speak on the defendant's behalf?" The Judge asked.

"Yes, your Honor. The defendant's mother, and his son's mother," Roman's lawyer said.

"Who would like to go first?" The Judge asked.

"Do you want to go first, Diva?" Roman's mother asked. Diva nodded her head, yes. "Yeah, I'll go."

"My daughter would like to speak first, your Honor," Marielle said. Not knowing that she was not allowed to address the Court.

"Fine, please take the stand and state your name, young lady," the judge told Diva.

"Are there any letters?" The judge asked Roman's lawyer.

"No, your honor," Samuel Sholar looked over at Roman. Roman looked over at him, squinted his eyes, and twisted his lips at his attorney.

"Oh, let me mention Mr. Edmonds that by expediting your sentencing you are waiving your presentence report to a later date. Do you understand and agree with that," the judge asked?

"Yes, ya Honor, that's fine," Roman said. His stomach turned. He really didn't want Diva and his mother to say anything in his behave. At this point whatever they would say to the court really wouldn't matter. The judge would not give him anything lesser than what was agreed upon in the plea deal. So them pleading and begging for mercy would be ineffective. Roman, himself, wanted to take the stand and tell the judge, DA and his lawyer, Sam Sholar, exactly what he thought about them and their system of so called Justice. In the back of his head, he wanted to get his money back from his crooked lawyer. It was obvious that he was working with the District Attorney. Maybe even fucking her. His eyes searched the courtroom for a way to escape. Then he thought about his son.

He would be thirteen years old when he got released. At that moment he was not calculating good time. He just thought about doing the entire ten years. Cocked sideways in his seat, his thumb was under his chin and his index finger rested against his temple. He watched as Diva walked to the stand, and took her seat.

"State your name, young lady, and speak your peace," the judge said.

"Devanna British, I'm Roman's baby momma..."

"Hmph, baby momma. Look at her ghetto ass," the DA said under her breath.

And I would like to say, FUCK THE DA, FUCK MY MAN'S LAWYER AND FUCK YOUR OLD MUTHAFUCKIN' ASS!" Diva thought to herself. It was what she really wanted to say to the people taking her man away from her.

"Your Honor despite what Roman is being convicted of he is a good man, and a great father. We all make mistakes, and that's what this is a mistake he made. I beg you, I BEG YOU! Please be lenient with him. I need him, my son needs him. There are way too many black kids growing up without their father's," Diva was trying to be strong, but couldn't. Tears streamed down her face, her lip trembled, and her heart hurt.

"It is so hard growing up where we're from. It's not easy living in our hood. We see people, our friends, our family members die on a weekly basis. And there are no jobs. When Roman got out of jail last time he tried to get a job but he couldn't. No one was willing to give him a chance because he had a felony." Diva wiped tears from her face with the back of her hand, "Snit, snit, ten years is sooo long ya Honor. What am I going to do? We were going to get married. He was changing. Please, ya Honor ... Snst, snst, don't give him ten years." The courtroom was quiet. The judged looked at Diva as she wiped more tears from her face. But the judge didn't feel any sympathy for her, Roman or his mother. If he could he would give Roman more time. He hated criminals, especially drug dealers.

Our Love Is A Life Sentence

They were the scum of the earth to him, "When you're done you can step down. Mrs. Edmonds, you can come up," the judge said.

On the way to the stand, Marielle, hugged Diva, "It'll be Okay, Diva." Was all she could say.

"Can you introduce yaself," Roman's lawyer said to his mother.

"Marielle Edmonds."

"What is your relationship to the defendant?"

"I'm his mother.

"Please explain to the court what you want to say on his behalf,"

"I stand here today as the 2014 Jackie Onassis Jefferson Award for my contributions to the community. But my life wasn't always this promising. I started selling drugs at the age of 14. I didn't stop until I was 46. I subjected my son to this lifestyle, so my heart is so heavy right now, snst ... Snst..."

Marielle began to cry.

As did Roman.

Two of the most important women in his life was in pain from what he was being sentenced for.

"...I'm ashamed that I didn't guide him in a better direction. What I know about selling drugs is that it is disease, just like using drugs is or drinking alcohol. It's not the last act that gets you in trouble, it's the first. One is too many, and a thousand is never enough. But I do know that through a program, I was able to get a better perspective on life and live my life differently for the last 14 years. I would just hope that the Court will show my son mercy today. I don't have anything else to say except I love you, Roman."

"I love you, too," Roman said.

"Mrs. Goldberg, do you have anything to say?" The judge asked the District Attorney as Roman's mother walked back to her seat in the pews.

"No, your Honor."

"Thank you for your input, Mrs. Edmonds. It was very heartfelt," the judge lied, "I've heard better sob stories," she thought to herself.

"Mr. Edmonds, would you like to speak?" The judge asked Roman. "Yes, ya Honor, I would," Roman said.

"Okay. You can say it from there. Speak into the microphone."

"Your Honor, I'd like to thank my family for coming. I've had a rough life. I've been abused, mentally and physically. Beat till I bled. I constantly ran away from home and slept in places that'll make you puke. Have you ever seen a man's brains blown out, ya Honor? I have. Have you ever tried stuff your best friend intestines back into his stomach after he's been shot? I have. I didn't want to be a drug dealer that's what the streets made me, that's what not being able to get a job has done to me. Don't get me wrong, there's no excuse for selling drugs, but the dope fiends and crack addicts aren't the only victims here. Growing up selling drugs I didn't care who I was hurting, but now I do. Seeing the damage that it does to my family, and other people and their families, ya Honor.

Before the indictment, I was changing my ways. I had stopped selling drugs...." it was Roman's turn to lie. He knew that he had stopped being heard on the wiretaps six months before the indictment. So, he used that information to his advantage.

"...I spoke out against violence at funerals, I spoke out against drugs. I helped a lot of people. When I made the decision to sell drugs again, I was going through a lot, bills, my son was being born, evictions and 11 couldn't get a job. I was goin through a lot. It's not an excuse. I just made a bad decision. I should have never done it, but I did and I'm willing' to take responsibility for that. But as far as the 851, I know it's part of the law, you know, but doing an extra five years for something I was already convicted for is more like double jeopardy, not justice, your Honor. It just hurts my family because I got kids to support. It's not Mrs. Goldberg's duty to support my kids. It's my responsibility as a man. An extra five years goes beyond just punishing me, it punishes my fiancé, my mother, my son. Thank you, your Honor."

"Thank you, Mr. Edmonds. Does either side like an opportunity to make any argument in aid of sentencing?" the judge asked.

"There are no arguments, your Honor," Roman's lawyer said.

"No arguments," your Honor," the District Attorney said.

"Sitting here before you, Mr. Edmonds, it is my sworn duty to impose a sentence that is sufficient but not greater than necessary to achieve the goals of sentencing. Pursuant to your plea agreement where you and the government agree that a sentence of 120 months was the appropriate sentence in this case and that I accepted that plea agreement, I believe it to be a reasonable sentence considering all the factors that I have taken into account, which is a very serious offense. You were a major trafficker of heroin and you say that you helped people, you also hurt them, and hurt the community, sir.

I have considered your history and characteristics. I understand that you had a very troublesome childhood, but for all the destruction that you have caused by selling this deadly drug, I truly believe that ten years is not enough. But I also believe that after you have served your debt to society you will be able to re-enter it and, hopefully, continue to be a loving father, and be with your family who has your best interest at heart and not those dope dealers, those individuals who you were involved with in the drug trafficking part of your life. The sentence you have agreed to is the sentence I impose today. It shows that there are harsh consequences for major drug trafficking so that it will promote for the law and also provide punishment for the serious crimes committed. Also, it is a sentence that will deter you from committing these types of acts again. Therefore, pursuant to the Sentencing Reform Act of 1984, it is my judgment that you, the defendant, Roman Edmonds, be committed to the custody of the Bureau of Prisons to be imprisoned for the term of 120 months.

CHAPTER 2 STREET CODE

AS ROMAN WAS HANDCUFFED and lead out of the courtroom, the cries of his girlfriend and mother hurt him to the core of his soul. He couldn't even look their way. Echoes of their torturous screams screeched through his mind outside of the courtroom. He clenched his fist and thought about his persecutors. The judge handed down his sentence and walked out of the courtroom without a care about his family. His glance over at the District Attorney's shitty smirk as she grouped her paperwork made his nostrils flare. His head overheated, his eyes turned bloodshot red. If he could he would kill them all for hurting his loved ones. He had killed in the past for lesser. His name being called by Diva as he walked out of the courtroom bounced around in his head. The words she and his mother said on his behalf, and his own words replayed in parts. in his head. He inhaled and exhaled as the elevator doors shut. He felt like a captured slave. Watching the Marshall push the elevator button to the lowest level made him feel as though he was being sent to hell.

Our Love Is A Life Sentence

As the elevator doors opened he could hear the voices of other would be slaves if it was the sixteenth century. It was 2013 and slavery was still going on. Black men were being captured at an alarming rate. Even dying in the process of being taken into captivity.

Back in his cell, he thought about the consoling hand his lawyer put on his shoulder after the judge handed down his lengthy sentence. His shoulder instantly shifted making Samuel Sholar's sweaty hand fall from his upper arm. He hated him. Samuel had played him out of a lot of money. Since his arrest, Roman had managed to keep his street business going through Diva. He had waited a few months before letting her know where his stash was, but eventually he had told her. At first, Diva was reluctant to help him sell the thousand bricks of heroin he stashed in the trunk of his old-school Dunk. It was put up at a storage garage that the Feds overlooked. After Roman explained that all she would have to do was pass the dope out and collect the money from his childhood friend, she agreed. Plus, she realized that her man would need a high priced lawyer to fight the case. So she carefully followed his instructions, retrieved the dope, and gave it to his friend two-hundred and fifty bricks at a time. Her trust in his friend, Dice, made it easier for her.

Our Love Is A Life Sentence

Dice had escaped the indictment thanks to his paranoia of cell phones. Him being able to go to Roman's house to get his work prevented him from having to discuss business over the phone. That along with Roman being a stand up nigga that lived by the code, helped him dodge the Federal Indictment. Of course, the Feds knew of him, and a few of Roman's co-defendants mentioned him during their proffer sessions, but without Roman's help, they didn't have enough information to indict him.

Dice sat around in fear waiting for the Feds to come get him, but that day never came. Sitting around without work for a few months hurt his pockets. Roman told him to chill, and he agreed to knowing that the Feds were probably watching him. "Just chill for' ah few, and I got you, bro-bro!" Roman told him. He trusted and loved Roman like a big brother so he did as he was told. When he got the call to come to Diva's house to pick up a gift Roman had got him for his birthday, he knew it was the work he had been waiting for. How did he know? Well, because Diva mentioned a birthday present in December, and his birthday wasn't until March. In his mind, he thought that it would be something small like fifty bricks, a little something to get him back on his feet. When he got home and saw that the backpack he took home was carrying two-hundred and fifty dope bricks, he almost cried. His man had come through for him once again.

While Roman was being sentenced, Dice was waiting on one of his runners to get back from Newark New Jersey with his work. Blonde was a thirty-year-old drug runner that played the part of a traveling gambler. She was a Caucasian female hustler that looked more like a school teacher than a mule.

Blonde had known Dice for close to two years. They met a couple of months before Roman got indicted, and they grew closer during the months that he fell back from the game. Being around her he observed her hustle and seen potential in her. She started small time, copping one or two bricks off him. Due to her consistency of keeping good work, her clientele grew, and she was now copping ten bricks a day. Knowing his situation, Blonde, took care of Dice until he got back on his feet.

She was a down ass bitch. So when Dice got back on his feet she was the first person he hit with work. He fronted her fifty bricks at first and charged her what he was paying per brick. But Blonde wasn't the only female hustler working for Dice. There was another chick named Evette. She was 5'2", and full of energy. A straight baller, and one dangerous woman to cross. She also had love and respect for Dice. He had got her out on bail one time when no one else would, and she wasn't even working for him at that time. Once she got out, she and Dice set up and robbed the nigga she was working for. The come up was a brick of coke and close to twenty thousand dollars.

Evette had gone on this trip, "Remember if you get pulled over..."

"...Don't let them search the car no matter what, especially, the trunk," Evette finished Dice's sentence. They had gone over what to say if she got pulled over by the police.

"If they ask you where you're on your way to, tell them Atlantic City to gamble. That'll explain the large amount of bread you got in the trunk. But they got no business searching the car. If it's just a traffic violation, take ya ticket, and just head back here. call the trip off. Do-not-go to Jers' if ya ass gets pulled ova. They'll try that nice approach, 'Ah miss., do you mind if we search ya car?' You tell 'em, 'Hell naw!" Dice said.

 "And make sure you circle the block a couple times before you bring the work into the spot. If you see any muthafuckas sitting in their car, don't stop, keep it moving," Dice went on to tell Evette.

Our Love Is A Life Sentence

"And finally, the most important of all only hit me on the new burn out. Do not hit me on ya working phone," he said.

Dice always brought two burn out phones for him and his courier every time they planned a trip. The burn out phones were to make sure they weren't doing business over tapped lines. "Nnn ... Nnn...Yo?!"

"I'll be Pullin' up in ah minute, fam'. I'ma circle the block like you said, and if shit's cool, I'll be in," Evette told Dice. Sitting his one burn out cell phone down, he picked up another. He had three in total; one for out of town moves that he destroyed after every trip; one for local dope moves and the other was for family and social purposes.

Dice picked up the one for family and social purposes and searched through his text messages. He screened through them as he pulled out a Newport, put it to his mouth and lit it. He blew smoke from his mouth and screened the messages for which ones he needed to delete. Scrolling through them he stopped and stared at a message Diva had sent him 10:21 am that morning. "They gave him ten. I'm droppin' mom off, and I'm going home," Diva texted.

"Ten years, FUCK!" He said, looking at the message, and studying it like the number of years Roman got was a typo. Then he shook his head, taking a pull from his cigarette.

Exhaling with his head tilted towards the ceiling, he thought about Diva and little Roman. "I'ma hold you down, homie!" He said as if he was talking to Roman.

Knock-knock ... Knock-knock.

Evette knocked on the door, and Dice let Evette in, "Sup 'Vette, how was the trip?"

"It was cool. I'm glad that shit's ova. Long as ride by myself, an' shit," Evette said, carrying two small duffle bags on each of her shoulders.

"That's the best way to do it, fam'." Dice said, snuffing out his Newport in a glass ashtray filled with several other crinkled cigarette butts and blunt roaches.

"Nigga, where the Loud at, I'm tryna get high," Evette said. That was another thing about taking that trip to New Jersey, Dice didn't want you getting high. The smell of weed was like a green-light for the cops to search your car. So, Dice prohibited using any drugs while on the trip.

"I got you," Dice said taking a seat on a cheap, green pleather coach, "Roll up, fam'," He said, pulling a sandwich bag of loud and a couple blunts out of the pouch of his hoodie, and throwing it on the inexpensive wooden living room table.

"Where that bitch, Blonde," Evette asked, looking around the small one-bedroom apartment located in the Greentree section of Pittsburgh. It was a spot Dice used just for their trips. The only furniture there was a cheap living room set, a TV, and a bed in the bedroom. Dice took his bitches there to fuck them sometimes, but he never stayed there.

Evette sat the duffle bags down on the wooden table, flopped down on the low-cost couch, and picked up the loud, and a blunt.

"She out makin' moves. She 'posed to be on her way here to get her work. How much you tryna get this time?" Dice asked Evette, unzipping one of the black duffle bags, pulling out a block of bricks wrapped in newspaper.

"At least twenty logs," Evette said. A log was ten bricks of heroin wrapped in newspaper horizontally.

"That's it?" Dice asked.

"Yeah, for now," Evette said.

Knock-knock. Knock-knock!

Nnn... Nnn...Nnn...

"...Get that. That's Blonde," Dice said, looking at a message displayed on his cell phone's LCD screen: "I'm at the door," the text read from Blonde.

"Wassup, bitch?!" Evette asked Blonde.

Blonde blew right past her, leaving Evette at the door, looking back towards Blonde, "What's wrong wit' you?" Evette asked, with a bitter look on her face.

"That nigga, Grinch, got me hot! He been owin' me three stacks fo' like ah week, an' shit. And now he duckin' me. Playin' games, an' shit!? Blonde said, taking a seat on the couch. A white person using the "N" word was against the rules in the hood, but Blonde wasn't considered white in the hood.
"See that's that bullshit niggas be on, cause we bitches niggas think they can get out on us. We ain't havin' dat shit, though! We gon' hav'tah deal with dat nigga, expeditiously!"
"Ha ha ha, expeditiously, huh? Let me try to take care of that," Dice said.
"Naw Dice, that make us look weak, an' shit"
"Vette, you just worry 'bout movin' that work. We don't need no heat. We can't make no money during a war," Dice explained. "Oh, it ain't gon' be no war," Evette said.
"Maaan, just chill," Dice said, taking a pull on the blunt. 'Evette fell back on the couch, with her lips twisted. She heard what Dice was saying, but she wasn't going to listen to him. She had her own plan's on how to settle the matter. Either Grinch paid up, or he was dead.

"I just want my ma'fuckin' money. I don't care how I get it," Blonde said, reaching for the blunt, "Let me hit that," she said to Dice.

INSIDE OF A CELL, at the Federal Courthouse, Roman, listened to a conversation two inmates were having from cell to cell. Fifteen minutes had passed since a third inmate walked past his cell on his way upstairs for his First Appearance. A First Appearance was a Court proceeding that told you a little bit about the charges you were being held on. The government presented a small portion of their evidence against you. They threw around the maximum mandatory minimum like twenty years and tried to convince the judge to hold you in jail until your trial. They told the Court how much of a menace to society you were, and most of the time the judge took that into consideration and held you over for Court. The only ones that really had a chance to make bail were the ones without drug cases or violence on their records.

Hearing chains clanking, Roman, sat up on his stainless-steel bench. The Marshall came to cuff and shackle them for transport back to (NEOCC), a Northeast Ohio Correctional Center in a small town on the outskirts of Youngstown, OH.

"What time you got, Marshall," Roman asked as he stood up, and approached the front of his cell.

"It's going on 4:00," the Marshall said, dropping some chains and some handcuffs, and shackles in front of his cell. As he kept walking he did the same in front of the other inmate's cells.

"Hey Marshall, we ain't go to court, yet," one of the unknown inmates said.

"They must've let Jay go," the other inmate said to his friend. "You'll be brought down tomorrow, or sometime this week."

"Aw man, that's bullshit," the inmate said.

"Hey, I don't make the rules, bud. I just following orders, come on out, and face the wall," the Marshall told him.

Being cuffed and shackled, Roman could get his first glance at the two inmates he listened to for several hours.

"They don't know what they're in store for," Roman thought.

Roman and one of the inmate's eyes met as a Marshall tugged on Roman's cuffs, "They're not too tight, are they?" The Marshall asked Roman.

"Nah, they cool," Roman said.

"Alright guys, let's go," One of the Marshall's said, and their captives marched to the elevator.

CHAPTER 3 FEDERAL HOLDING

IN THE BACK OF THE TRANSPORT VAN,
"Where they takin' us, dawg?" The inmate that caught Roman's eye: him. The inmate looked to be around twenty-three, twenty-four years old. He wore a white V-neck t-shirt and True Religion jeans.

"A federal holding in Youngstown," Roman said.

"Up in Ohio?" The inmate said.

"Yea-yup," Roman answered.

"Yo, where you from. Look like I know you," The other inmate asked.

 "The West," Roman said.

"Where at on the West?" The inmate asked.

"G-Way "

"My man's from over there. He lives in Cherry Court. You know 'Bout It, that's my dawg. We were up Shuman Juvenile Facility together."

"Yeah, that's my young boy."

"What's ya name, dawg?" The other inmate asked.

"Roman."

"Oh, I heard of you," Was all the inmate said, but he knew much more about Roman.

"Where y'all from?" Roman asked.

"I'm Banks, I'm from Larimer, and dis my man Smooth, he from Manchester," The inmate said.

"They just pick y'all up today, huh?" Roman asked, knowing the answer to his question. He knew they had just got picked up because of the street clothes they had on, and by the conversation he overheard them having. But Roman had never heard of either one of them, and he knew ballers from both sections of Pittsburgh they were from.

"How many of y'all got locked up?" Roman asked.

"Six, but they let everybody go but us. They'll probably let us go tomorrow," Banks said.

"These ma'fuckas is vicious. Y'all got any drug cases on y'all's record or any violence?"

"Shit! I gotta ma'fuckin' case pending. Ah lil brick joint," Smooth said.

"Pss, they goin try to keep you. They gon' say you're a threat to the community. You been going to ya court hearings?" Roman asked.

"Yeah, every last one. I just got my shit postponed like ah month ago," Smooth said.

"Oh, you might be aight then. Y'all talked to Pretrial Services?" Roman asked.

"Pretrial Services?" Smooth was puzzled.

"Yeah, before y'all go to y'alls first appearance somebody will ask y'all questions like if you ever been locked up, ya income..." yeah, we talked to them," Smooth said.

"What's up with them?" Banks asked.

"They play a big part in ya release. like ya man, normally, they wouldn't let him out, but being he's been showing up to his Court hearings they might let him go. That shit shows that you're not a threat, and you'll come to Court," Roman told them.

"That's wassup," Smooth said.

"What about you, fam'. You got any old cases," Roman asked Banks.

"Nah, dis my first time being locked up," Banks said.

"Okay now, let me ask y'all this; who's at the head of the indictment," Roman asked.

"Head of the indictment," Banks asked. The two. young hustlers were lost, much like Roman when he first got locked up.

"Yeah, that paper your hand is ya Indictment. It got a list of names on it, and what y'alls charges is. Who's at the top of the list," Roman asked.

"Yo! They got me on the top. What that mean?" Banks asked with a nervous look on his face.

"Damn fam', you might not be goin' home. They rarely let the head of the Indictment out on bail," Roman told Banks the bad news. "Unless they rattin'," Roman thought.

"Bro, dat is crazy! So, you saying is I might not be goin' nowhere?" Banks restated.

"I don't know, it depends. You ain't got no record so you might skate," Roman said.

IN THE CRAFTON HEIGHTS SECTION OF PITTSBURGH, Diva and little Roman walked into their home, "Come on, Roman. So you can eat, and get in the tub," Diva told her son. She had stopped at Wendy's and got them something to eat, so she wouldn't have to cook. With everything that happened, she didn't feel like it. As Diva sat the Wendy's bags, little Roman's book bag, and her purse on the living room table, her phone rung.

Cling-a-ling-a-ling ... Cling-a-ling-a-ling!

Searching through her purse she hurried to answer the call. She was hoping that it was Roman, but it wasn't. It was another one of her so called friends, "Bitch just tryna be nosey!" Diva said under her breath. Several of her friends had called. Most of them just wanted to know what happened at Court, but there was only one person she wanted to hear from, and that was Roman. Sitting her phone down she turned on the Cartoon Network for little Roman, and prepared his food for him, "Here you go, baby. Come eat," she said to little Roman, watching him play with a toy from the meal.

AT (NEOCC) IN NORTHEAST OHIO 6:03 pm, the transport van pulled up to the guarded gate at the back entrance of the Federal Holding Facility and stopped at the gate. Two guards walked down each side of the van with mirror sticks, checking the bottom of the van for any explosives as a shotgun toting guard watched. Once the van was cleared, the gate lifted, and the van drove into the lot of the prison. After a few seconds of hearing guards talk, the back of the van opened, 'Wight guys, come on out. Watch ya step," one of the transporting officers said.

One by one, Roman and the other two inmates climbed out of the van. Outside of the van stood several guards and a White Shirt. A White Shirt is a superior officer.

"Okay, state ya name and number's. If you don't have a number just state ya name and birthdays," the White Shirt said, looking down at a packet of information and photocopied photographs of each inmate on a clipboard.

"Roman Edmonds #3-2-5-5-4-0-6-8," Roman went first.

"Ross Farrier, 2-17-1990," Smooth stated.

"Ellis Reeves Jr., 5-14-1989," Banks stated.

The White Shirt looked at each photograph and inmate and was positive that he had the right inmates. Aight, follow me," the White Shirt said, lead them to receiving.

Our Love Is A Life Sentence

Walking down the prison corridor, Roman, Banks, and Smooth walked carefully so that the chains and shackles clamped around their ankles wouldn't trip them up.

Being that Roman had been there for two years he was already in the prison's system. So, he would be allowed to go back to his unit, but Banks and Smooth would sit around for several hours to be processed.

Inside of a small room in receiving, the inmates had their handcuffs and shackles removed, and was stripped search, and giving prison uniforms. Each of them went into an enclosed makeshift cubicle for privacy where they stripped down. Roman removed his court uniform, t-shirt, and underwear, and stood naked before the guard, "Open ya mouth ... Move ya tongue around ... Turn around ... Let me see the bottom of your feet, and bend over and cough," The guard commanded, and Roman complied, "Get dressed. They got your supper on the unit. Ask the guard for it when you get there. What unit you on?" The guard asked Roman.

"B-block," Roman. said.

"Go head, and head back," the guard told Roman.

"Aight," coming out of the cubicle, Roman seen the Banks and Smooth being lead into a cell, "I'll see y'all niggas on the compound, Roman said.

'Wight," Banks said.

"Yeah, Okay, cool. I'll holler at you, bro," Smooth said. After passing through a few barred gates, Roman reached B-block. Seeing Roman at the door the C.O. working the unit buzzed him in, "Edmonds, you got mail, and I got ya dinner tray," the C.O. working the unit said.

Roman got his mail and his tray and sat it on an empty table on his way to his cell.

"You don't want dat, Roman?" An inmate asked.

"Naw, that's you. Go 'head," Roman told the scruffy old white inmate. Looking around the Unit, Roman got a couple head nods from inmates he fucked with. Knowing he had just been sentenced they let him be for the time being. They all related to the feeling of being sentenced unjustly and being held down at court all day. It was very draining and stressful.

"Hmph, here fo' ten ma'fuckin' years," Roman said under his breath as he glared at the convicts playing dominoes, working out and watching TV.

Our Love Is A Life Sentence

INSIDE OF HIS CELL, Roman's celly, Barry, was making a pizza for them, "Wassup fam', you give them dirty ma'fuckas ah piece of ya mind before they threw the book at you?" Barry asked.

"You know I did, ha ha," Roman said, trying to fight off the pain he felt inside. "I'll tell you all about it after I call Diva," Roman told his celly, putting his mail on, the bed, and grabbing his phone book.

"Might, I'm makin' us a pizza. I know ya hungry," Barry said.

"Hell yeah," Roman said, on the way out of his cell.

"Don't forget we got Love & Hip Hop tonight at eight," Barry said.

"Oh, yeah. I forgot about dat shit," Roman replied, glancing down at the four phones on the Unit. "Yo! Hol' dat phone, fam," Roman yelled to an inmate hanging up the phone he was using.

"Let me-get dat," another convict named Big Stan said, trying to grab the phone from the inmate holding it tightly.

"Roman's about to use dis. He just came back from gettin' sentenced," the scrawny inmate said.

"I don't give ah fuck! Fuck dat nigga!" Big Stan said, snatching the phone out of the inmate's hand.

"Dat's me, fam," Roman walked up and said.

Our Love Is A Life Sentence

"Man, you betta get da fuck outta here," Big Stan said, turning his back to Roman, and putting the phone to his ear. Seeing what was going on Roman's homies started to activate. Getting up out of their seats. An inmate on Roman's tier told his celly about what was going on, and Barry stepped out of his cell. But Roman put his hands up and calmed the situation. Just as he did so another phone became available, "Here you go, Roman. Get on dis one. Fuck dat nigga. Nigga think he tough an' shit," the convict said, handing Roman the phone. Nobody on the unit liked Big Stan. He had been there for three weeks and was trying to run the unit already. He knew that Roman was a shot-caller on the blocks but because he was bigger than Roman, he felt that he could try him, and get away with it.

After a few attempts to call someone, Big Stan hung up the phone, "I don't know why y'all niggas keep trying me. I'ma fuck, one of you bitch ma'fuckas up, straight up!" Big Stan said, staring Roman in the eyes as he walked past him. Roman just smiled at him, punching in the digits of his prepaid calling card.

"Get the fuck out dat seat, man," Big Stan walked over to the TV and said to another inmate sitting comfortably, watching the previous episode of Love & Hip Hop.

"There's a seat right there, Stan," the inmate said.

"SMMMAACCCK!! Well, go sit in it ma'fucka, and the next time you call me Stan I'ma really fuck you up. You betta put 'Big,' in front of dat shit. Address me right., nigga!" Big Stan said after he hauled off and smack the shit out of the inmate back talking to him. The smack got the attention of the Unit. Even the C.O. working the Unit noticed the shift in tension in the Unit, but he put his, head back down into his Newspaper.

"...Thank you for using Metro Prepaid calling," the automatic calling card service.

"Hey," Roman said into the phone.

"Hiiii, husband! I just got ya son out of the tub, "Say hi to ya dad, Roman," Diva told little Roman.

"Hey, lil man. What you doin'?" Roman asked.

"Say hi, Roman," Diva encouraged her three year old to say, hi."

"Dada ... Hi daddy ... Daddy, I had McDonald's," Little Roman said.

"You had McDonald's, lil man?"

"You okay, husband?" Diva asked.

"Naw, question is, is you a'ight?!" Roman said.

"You know you gotta soldier fo' ah wife. Fuck dem! They can't break us, weak ma'fuckas!!"

"Ha ha ha, I love my wifey," Roman said with a laugh.

"You know it's me and you fo'eva, husband. It's whateva! I don't give ah fuck how much time they give you. I don't care if they give you life. I'm right here, and I'ma be right here. Our love is ah life sentence. We locked in fo' life, husband!"

"We locked in fo' life, daddy," little Roman repeated what he heard his mother say.

"Ha ha ha..."

"Ha ha ha, we got straight soldiers ova here. Aw, dat's crazy!" Hearing the voices of his family made Roman feel invisible. Their love and support would be all he needed to get through his bid.

"He just like his dad, straight soldier," Diva said, kissing their son, "Mmmuuu-ah! Love you, lil Roman," she told her son.

"What about me," Roman asked, jokingly.

"I love you, too, big head," Diva said.

"YOU HAVE TWO MINUTES REMAINING ON THIS CARD," the automatic calling card service reminded the couple.

"Shut up, bitch. I can't stand her ass, ha ha ha," Diva said with a laugh. She was talking about the voice recording that reminded the couple of how many minutes they had remaining on the calling card.

"I know, right, ha ha," Roman agreed with his ride or die chick. "So am I goin' to see y'all tomorrow," Roman asked.

"You sure are," Diva said.

"Aight, I'll see y'all tomorrow. Love y'all," Roman told Diva, feeling: a sadness setting in the pit of his stomach.

"No! 'Don't go, husband."

"Thank you fo' holdin' me down, wifey. I..."

...*CLICK!*

The phone call disconnected just as Roman was going to tell Diva he loved her again.

Looking at his watch, Roman, seen that he had time to shower and get ready for Love & Hip Hop. Walking by the TV and other inmates sitting around it, he looked at the back of Big Stan's head.

"Look at dis nigga, all comfortable and shit," Roman thought on his way up to his cell.

After showering, Roman and his celly heated up their pizza's in the unit's microwave. When they got to the seats in front of the TV, two inmates got up behind Big Stan so they could sit down showing that they had the juice on the block!

"Thanks homie," Roman told the inmate getting up for him to sit down.

"It's all good. You know what it is, homie," the inmate said.

Hearing Roman's voice, Big Stan turned around. He was letting Roman know he knew that he was behind him. Glancing back at Roman, Big Stan gritted at him, "Some of y'all bitch ass ma'fuckas should be payin' tah watch TV in dis bitch. I'ma start chargin' yaw ma'fuckas!" Big Stan said. He had gotten away with the phone incident, and now he was seeing just how far he could go. If he could put Roman in his place he knew that a lot of other convicts would fall in line.

Hearing what Big Stan was saying, Barry, looked over at Roman, but Roman just kept pouring his Pepsi into his plastic cup he wasn't paying either of them any attention. "LAST WEEK ON LOVE & HIP HOP," the television blared as Roman bit into his pizza and sat back. Chewing his pizza another convict watched Roman, and waited for a response to Big Stan's statement Roman looked the man in his eyes, and nodded once the inmate that was watching him then turned back around and got into the reality show like everyone else "Look at Stevie, dat nigga crazy'" He said, sparking up other comments from the other inmates and convicts watching the show.

CHAPTER 4 YOU GON' RESPECT ME

BEFORE NINE O'clock count, three new inmates entered B-block, and one of them was Smooth. Unfortunately, he was moved into Big Stan's cell. "Aw naw, fuck dat! Ma'fucka ain't movin' in my shit!" Big Stan said, watching as Smooth was entering his cell.

Roman watched as Big Stan tried to persuade the Officer to move Smooth to another cell. "There's no other place to move him. He's stuck with you until another cell opens up," the Officer told him.

"Man, dis is some bullshit!" Big Stan said, stomping off to his cell.

"COUNT TIME... COUNT TIME. ALL INMATES RETURN TO YOUR CELL'S FOR NINE O'CLOCK COUNT," an announcement came over the prison PA system.

"Lil dude came back wit' me," Roman told Barry, walking to their cell.

"You gon' get him outta there?" Barry asked Roman.

"I'ma see what I can do," Roman said, following Barry into their cell, and clicking their cell door shut for count.

Our Love Is A Life Sentence

CLICK-CLICK ... CLICK-CLICK ... CLICK-CLICK. Simultaneously, cell doors. on B-block clicked open, " almost an hour later.

"COUNT CLEAR ...COUNT CLEAR," a C.O. announced over the P.A. system.

Soon as the door kicked open, Roman, came out of his cell and started walking in the direction of Big Stan's cell. On the way there the convict that gave him the head nod during Love & Hip Hop, handed him a 10" shank as he passed him. The closer Roman got to Big Stan's cell, the more of his associates followed him. It seemed as though everyone on the cell block, except Big Stan, knew that he was about to be dealt with for his blatant disrespect.

By the time Roman reached Big Stan's cell at least a dozen of his associates were behind him. When he got there Smooth was coming out of his cell, "Was ... Up" Smooth tried to speak to Roman but was swiftly swept to the side by Barry.

Looking at the entourage behind Roman he knew something serious was going down as did the other inmates looking up at the small crowd of goons entering Big Stan's cell. The small crowd even caught the eyes of the C.O. working the unit, but when he saw whose cell they were entering he turned a blind eye. He didn't even like Big Stan.

53

He saw the way he took advantage of the smaller inmates and hated it. Seeing the convicts apart of the swarm of homies the C.O. knew Roman was leading the pack. Smooth looked back as the convicts entered his cell and then blended with the other inmates headed to the lower level of the cell-block.

"Nigga, wassup wit' dat disrespectful shit you been on?!!" Roman asked, displaying his jailhouse knife made of cold, stiff metal.

"YO?! Roman, man ... Yo, hol' up!" Big Stan tried to keep his composure as he pleaded for a chance to give Roman an explanation, "Bruh, I'm goin' through a lot. You know how these crackers have you," Big Stan said, registering his odds in his head. He could take a couple of them. He might even take out Roman but if he attempted to but he knew he would surely die. Nine times out of ten when an inmate saw a shiv he was about to die. So, Big Stan's heart pumped with fear, and his breath became scarce. He could barely talk, gasping for air between his words. Suddenly he thought about his daughter.

Without saying another word, Roman sprung into action. Leaping forward, he threw a combination of punches. One punch landed in Big Stan's gut, another across his eye, backed by an uppercut from Roman's knife bearing hand.

Before Big Stan knew it, he had landed on his ass and Roman was holding his knife under his throat, drawing a small trickle of blood.

"Nigga, the next time you get outta pocket, you gon' die in dis ma'fucka!" Roman said, through clenched teeth.

And just as suddenly as they came, Roman and his boys were gone.

Still dazed, Big Stan felt the small puncture wound leaking from under his chin. Then he put his hands to his face, "Thank you for saving my life, Lord," he said, thanking his God for giving him a second chance.

 "I gotta call my daughter," he said, gathering himself from his cell's chipped painted floor. Looking in the mirror he shook his head at the sight of a bloody chin and swollen eye.

ON THE EMPTY ROADS OF CRAFTON HEIGHTS, Dice's Black GMC Terrain traveled on its way to Diva's house. Although the streets of the West Side seemed quiet he knew that the evil's that be lurked in the shadows of its darkness. It was a quarter to eleven, and at this time of night jackers and police waited in the depths of the abyss waiting to prance on their victim's like the predators they were.

With his head on swivel, Dice, held his hand on the 40 Caliber sitting in his lap. Crafton Heights was a hot spot especially in the section he was in but, "It's better to be caught with it than without it," was his mentality.

Squinting his eyes, he attempted to see who was pulling up behind him at a stop sign. Their headlights momentarily blinded him. As he slowly drove ahead, the car behind him made a right. The occupant driving the vehicle was a middle aged white man. Seeing the white driver reminded him that he had crossed from the ghetto section of Crafton Heights into the white section where Diva lived.

Hitting a combination of gears and buttons Dice's stash box opened. Putting his street sword on his hip, he took out a small package that contained Loud, Cocaine, and Heroin, and put it in the pouch of his hoodie.

Our Love Is A Life Sentence

After dialing Diva's cellphone number, he put his cellphone to his ear, and climbed out of his SUV, "Open the door, I'm out front," he told Diva.

After opening the door, Diva, fell into Dice's arms, "Agh ... Agh... Agh ... Agh, they took him... They took him fo' ten long years, Dice," she cried.

"Shit gon' be a'ight, Dee," Dice consoled Diva, wrapping her tightly into his arms.

Snst ... Snst..

"I hate them ma'fuckas!" Diva said', stepping back to allow Dice to enter her home, "Come on she said, walking away from the door.

Dice stepped into the house and shut and locked the door behind him. Removing the hoodie from his head he watched Diva's ass sway side-to-side as he followed her into the living room, "You want some Henny?" Diva asked falling into the couch.

"Nah, I'm straight. Oh, you in her watchin' Belly an' shit, huh?" Dice said, seeing DMX on the large television screen.

"Yeah, dis my shit. Here, light up," Diva handed Dice a pre-rolled blunt.

"FLICK—FLICK—SWOOSH!" The lighter top ignited, flickering a burning flame that set the Exotic Marijuana a

flame, "Whew!" Dice blew the flame out and took a few pulls of the blunt. Blowing the partially translucent white vapors into the air he watched it as the smoke separated and disappeared, "Where you get this, damn," Dice asked.
"That boy Ew-Wee. He got that fire!" Diva told Dice.
"Hell yeah. I gotta holla at ol' boy. This shit's betta than what he sold me last night," Dice said, taking a few more puffs of the Exotic, and handing the blunt to Diva. "And I gotta holla at his man's Grinch," Dice added.
"Why, what's up wit' him?"
"He owes Blonde some bread, and he keeps try'na play her." "Nah, we can't have that. She sellin' our shit, right?"
"Yea-yup."
"Yeah, deal wit' that shit. We can't have ma'fuckas out here thinking we playin' wit' 'im," Diva said, inhaling the Exotic.
"Oh, I got 'im. Best believe that!" Dice said, pulling out the package of product from his hoodie pouch.
"Let me grab the shit," Diva said, seeing Dice pull out the product. Ew-Wee was the weed man on the West Side and Grinch was a close associate of his. They had all grown up together, but they all hung in different circles that got money. Ew-Wee and Grinch knew Dice's reputation and knew he wasn't to be fucked with. So, Dice felt that it was

only a matter of him hollering at Grinch for him to give him Blonde's money.

"I talked to Roman about an hour ago," Diva said, making her way out of the kitchen with a box of sandwich bags and a bag of long balloons.

How he holdin' up?"

"He seems to be in good spirits. He knows I'm here and ain't goin nowhere."

"That's wassup It ain't nothin' like havin' ah soldier do ya bid wit' you."

"Didn't you meet Alex while you were locked up?" Alex was Dice's girlfriend Alexandria Baker.

"Yeah. She soldiered fo' me. Rode the last two years of my three-year bid out wit' me, and I've been wit' her eh' since."

"And you've been faithful?"

"Well, you know ... Come on, sis'! Ha ha ha ... Put it this way, I know where home's at."

"Whhewww," Diva blew smoke from her mouth, and sat the baggies and balloons on the living room table, "Damn! I forgot the Vaseline and tape," Diva said, passing Dice the blunt.

After going back into the kitchen Ear the Vaseline and tape, Diva, sat down at the table.

"You gotta let me get ah blunt of this. This shit here, whheww ...This shit here is bananas," Dice said, inhaling and exhaling more vapors into the air.

"Got you I gotta dub sack fo' you," Diva said, taking the product out of its package.

First, Diva spread each of the narcotics across the bottom of separate sandwich bags and rolled them tightly. Then she rolled them together in another sandwich bag, and folded the work in two, and stuffed that into a balloon, and tied it. Then she took two fingers and scooped out a glob, of Vaseline and lubricated the balloon. After she did that she put another baggie around the balloon full of work, tied it, and then stuffed it in a second balloon, "What. that look like," she asked Dice.

Try to make it as tight as you could. We don't want that nigga having no problems putting it up his ass," Dice replied. So Diva wrapped tape around the work to compress it even more "Damn, this shit's crazy. Niggas don't want bitches playin' wit' they asses, but would put something like this up they ass to get work in the prison," Diva said, stuffing the work in its final balloon, and tying the end, into a tight little knot.

"Not me! I used to swallow my shit. But hey, to each his own. It's whatever's clever. Eh'body play they part different."

"Yeah, you right," Diva said, sitting the small vibrator sized package on the table.

"Sam don't got no problems with running this last package in, does he?" Dice asked about Roman's lawyer... He knew about him taking drugs into the jail to one of Roman's homies. It had been going on for over a year.

"He bet' not have a problem wit' it after what happened today. But naw, tho, after a talk he had wit' Roman he was gon' run the PK in fo' free, but I told him, it was cool," Diva said

"Why' That ma'fucka owe Roman."

"I know but I don't want him throwing shit up in my man's face."

"Hmph, yeah? Well, tell my dude I send snitch-proof love and hit me if he needs me," Dice said, extending his arms to give Diva a hug.

"Here, take this... I'll get more tomorrow," Diva said. At the door, she handed Dice a baggie of Khalifa, a strand of Exotic Buds named after the Pittsburgh rapper Wiz Khalifa. The two blunts she had ready-rolled in her bedroom was enough to get her through the rest of the night, and the next morning.

Our Love Is A Life Sentence

BACK AT (NEOCC), Roman and three of his homies sat around playing dominoes, "How much we need?" Roman asked, the scorekeeper.

"Y'all need fifty, and we need seventy-five," said the scorekeeper. "Sixes," Roman called out, and Barry laid the double-sixes.

"Give me twenty," Roman's other competitor called out After studying the board, Roman played five four. Smooth stood behind him, and 'shook his head about the bone Roman decided to play.

"Give us twenty," Roman's competitor said, laying the five-three bone.

"Give me twenty-five," Barry said, slamming the double-five bone down on the metal table covered with a cream-colored blanket.

"What's score?" Roman asked, feeling threatened in a sense. He was hoping the scorekeeper didn't have the blank-five bone.

"Y'all need five, and we need, thirty," the scorekeeper said, looking over his hand for the right bone to play. Just as Roman feared, the scorekeeper brought the blank-five crashing to the table, "Give me twenty' We need ten, and y'all still need five," the scorekeeper said, writing down the new score.

Our Love Is A Life Sentence

"Fuck!" Roman said under his breath Barry looked over at him. "Don't look over at Roman fo' help, nigga yaws asses are in trouble. Come on partner, let's get they asses up'" Roman's competitor said.

"Damn pot 'na, ol' boy talkin' cash shit," Roman said, looking at the bones in his hand, "What you say we needy?" Roman asked again.

"You know what you need. He den tol'cha ass three times," Roman's competitor said.

SWWOOO-SLLLAAMMM

" GIVE US THE SAME TWENTY, NIGGA. SEE IT'S YA MOUTH. IT'S YA MOUTH. NIGGA!"

Hahaha.

Roman slammed the double-blank on the table and got the same scoring points as the scorekeeper.

"Why duck you played da blank-five? You know they only needed five. Damn!" Roman's competitor said, criticizing the scorekeeper's decision to take the money, oppose to passing it up.

"Wassup wit' you?" Roman asked Smooth, walking away from the domino table as his competitors argued-aver the scorekeeper's last play.

"Chillin'. What was up wit' my celly, bra?" Smooth asked.

"Ah lil some'in' happened earlier that I thought he might want to talk about, but it's cool, though," Roman told Smooth.

"Bro, I ain't try'na be in no cell wit' ah nigga you beefin' wit', you know?" Smooth told Roman, hitting his fist to the palm of his hand and his head bouncing sideways.

"I got you. My celly should be gettin' transferred any day now, might be tonight. If he don't, I'll work some'in out fo' you. Shit though, you might not even be here that long. You got a good shot of gain' home, fam'. You call ya people yet?"

"Nah, I gotta get a calling card or some'in'."

"Oh yeah, I gotta ah few joints fo' you. I meant to give you these joints when I came down.

"Thanks, bro. Good look. How I use this joint though?"

"Just dial ya number, and when they ask you fo' the card number just punch in the number on the card.

"Bet!" Smooth said, headed to the phones.

Roman thought about calling Diva again. He normally did but being she was coming to visit the next day he decided to wait to talk to her."

Not long after Smooth finished his phone call, all inmates were locked in for the night.

Our Love Is A Life Sentence

"We'll talk in the morning. You going to breakfast?" Roman asked Smooth on the way to their cells.

"Yeah. What time they call it?" Smooth asked.

"Around 5:30-6:00," Roman told Smooth.

"Make sure I'm up, bro."

"Got you," Roman said, stepping into his cell, and clicking the cell door shut.

***

"STEVENS? STEVENS?!" A Correctional Officer's voice called out over the intercom built into the cell's wall. Hearing his last name, Barry jumped down from the top bunk, and pressed a button on the intercom, "Yeah?!"

"It's three o' clock, you got an hour to get your things together. You're being transferred. If you want to take a shower, go ahead. Just be downstairs with everything ten minutes to four," the officer said.

'Wight, thanks ... Bro, I'ma hit this light," Barry told Roman before clicking the light in the cell on.

"Go 'head, fam'! Damn, you outta here," Roman said. After being sentenced every inmate was transferred to their home jail, NEOCC was just a hold over jail where inmates waiting to be tried and sentenced.

Our Love Is A Life Sentence

After Barry gathered the things he was taking with him, he took a shower and sat to talk with Roman. "Bro, make sure you get at me," he told Roman.

"Shit fam', you get out before me. You make sure you get at me," Roman said, smiling at his celly.

"You know I'ma holla. I got the address, I'ma hit you once ah month.

"That's wassup, homie..."

"Stevens, you ready?" The officer asked over the intercom.

"Love you, bro!" Barry said, as the cellmates shook hands and hugged.

"Love you, too," Bro-ski," Roman said, feeling a sadness overcoming him.

"Bro, you'll be outta here before you know it. Then you can start biddin', you know?" Barry said, exiting the cell.

"Yeah, they should designate next week. I should be gone in two," Roman explained to his man. Barry was two years younger than him but he carried himself as if he was much older. The two men had gotten close even though Barry was from Cleveland, and Roman was from Pittsburgh. Clicking his cell door shut, Roman, watched as Barry, and a few other inmates were lead out of the unit.

"Holla, homie," Roman said in a whisper, his breath putting a light fog on the cell door window from his closeness to it.

After watching his man walk out of the unit's front door, Roman clicked the cell light off, went to his bunk and fell back onto his pillow. Thoughts raced through his head. He felt defeated... Although he was still making money and was able to do his time comfortably, he still felt a sense of losing everything. The more he thought, the more his heart pounded, faster and faster. He felt a burning sensation in his nose, and one-by-one, tears streamed down the sides of his face. A wetness drew on his pillow from his tears settling on the cotton fabric of the pillow case.

"Ten fuckin' years, tho! Fuck, man! I hate these muthafuckas! I hate these muthafuckas," he repeated. His insides filled with hate. He wished he could get revenge. He thought of ways that he could pay back the judge, DA, and his lawyer.

Yes, it was true that his lawyer brought him drugs, and was helping both of them stay afloat,
but that was nothing compared to being home with Diva and his son. Wiping the tears from his face, he rolled over and glared at the family portrait of Diva, his son, and himself. He could barely' see the details of the portrait in

Our Love Is A Life Sentence

the dark, but he had stared at it so much that their images were etched in the back of his mind.

Rolling back over unto his back, he got up, and got himself ready for chow. After pissing, brushing his teeth, and washing his face, he thought about moving Smooth in to his cell, and schooling him on the things that needed to be said to the judge for him to make bail.

CHAPTER 5 LET'S MAKE MOVES

The time was close to 9:00 am, Diva, had woke up for the second time that morning. The first time Little Roman's cries woke her up. He had sluggishly made his way into his mother's bedroom with his sippy-cup in his mouth. She tried to ignore him, but seeing she wasn't getting up to tend to his whining, Little Roman climbed up on the bed and tugged at his mother. After his failed attempt to wake her, he paused and studied his mother's face. Then Diva, with her eyes still closed, smiled, and this let Little Roman know that she was awake.

"Hmph! Hmph!" He hit her on the arm, Diva, still played sleep, but she giggled. This made her son mad, "Ma. Maaa. Maaaa! !" Little Roman whined.

"Hm... Hm..Hm," Diva silently chuckled, still not opening her eyes.

Clunk!

"Ouch, boy!" Little Roman threw his sippy-cup at his mother's, hitting her in the head.

"Hm ... Hm ... Hm ... Hm," now it was Little Roman's turn to laugh. Diva smiled back at her son, and pulled him down to her bosom, You hungry?" She asked.

"Mrn-hm," Little Roman grunted, and shook his head up-and-down, accepting his sippy-cup back from his mother and putting it in his mouth.

"You wanna go over Grandma Marielle's and see ya aunt Syria?" Diva asked her son.

"Mm-hm," little Roman grunted, sitting up and looking his mother in the eyes. He loved being over his Grandma Marielle's with her, and his aunt Syria.

After fixing her son something to eat, Diva, looked at the time on her phone, it read 7:01 am. Sitting Little Roman in his room, she placed his food in front of him, put on his favorite Elmo DVD, and went back to sleep for a couple hours.

Now it was 9:00 am, and she knew she had to get up. Wiping coal from her eye, she looked at her cell phone, and replied to a few phone calls and text messages. One in particular was from Roman's sister, Syria.

Pressing send, she called his sister back, "Hey... Yea...Okay. I'll be there soon," Diva said, confirming that she still wanted his sister to watch Little Roman while she went on her visit.

Then Diva went to the text messages between Roman's lawyer, Samuel, and herself.

TEXT MESSAGES:

DIVA TO SAMUEL SHOLAR: I'll be at Starbucks@10:00 am.

SAMUEL SHOLAR TO DIVA: I'll be there.

After a few minutes, Samuel Sholar, replied. He was already at his office located Downtown Pittsburgh. He wanted to get this last trip out of the way, so he could finally be done with the whole ordeal.

"I'll be gone for a few hours on a lawyer-client visit for a few hours, foward my messages to my email, and I'll monitor my calls," The attorney told his office administrator, leaving his firm.

Ten came fast. Diva got ready for her visit, smoked a blunt, dropped Little Roman off, and was at Starbucks ordering a large cup of Joe. After getting her order, she went into the bathroom and dumped it out in the sink. Looking around, she made sure that she was the only one in the bathroom, pulled the balloon wrapped package from her panties and put it in the cup, along with twenty fifty dollar bills.

Walking out of the bathroom, Diva spotted Samuel, and walked over to the table where he sat, "Hey!" She said, taking a seat, and sitting her cup on the table.

"Tell Roman I will be putting in for his appeal today. It's what he wants, but I'ma be a hundred percent honest with you, Diva, he's not going to get any relief." Samuel said, delivering the bad news to Diva about the appeal Roman requested.

"Why you say that? That's some real negative shit to say, Sam."

"Well, because the plea is a binding plea that he agreed to and the judge accepted. The only grounds he would have for an appeal is the ineffective counsel approach, and that's going to be denied because he said in the sentencing transcript's that I did a good job to the judge."

"Hmph! Just do what he tells you to do. I need him to be as happy as he could possibly be."

"Well, this is my last rodeo, he'll be at a different jail soon," Samuel said, taking a sip of his iced coffee.

"It doesn't have to be. Roman has friend's that will still be there. Like the guy you're taking the stuff to, he still hasn't been to court yet," Diva responded.

"Ah, this is it for me, Diva," Samuel said, shaking his head, 'No,' but not knowing if he wanted the easy money to end.

He was making two-to-four thousand a month from their arrangement.

Without Roman running the show he knew that there would be a chance of error, and error was something he could not afford as an attorney. One slip up could cost him his career, or even worse, get him a lengthy prison sentence.

Sitting in his car at a paid parking lot, Samuel, took the dildo-shaped package from the large coffee cup. Holding it with his fingers he shook the water off it and wiped it with a paper towel. Removing his legal documents from his attaché, he removed a false bottom from it and placed the package inside of it. Then he put the false bottom back inside of his briefcase and covered it with his folder's and papers.

As Diva and Samuel, separately, made their ways to NEOCC for visits, Evette, rode around her Sheradan neighborhood making drug sells.

Jumping out of her 2005 Lexus ES 330, she ran into a corner store in the hood. Inside there was a small line of three, and at the head of the line was just the man she wanted to see. Grinch pulled out a D-boy knot and paid for his blunts and snacks.

Compared to her 5'2" frame, Grinch was a giant to her, but that wasn't going to stop her from stepping to him. Evette had a heart of a lioness and was preparing to pounce on her prey. Tapping her waistline, she checked for her .380. Nodding her head up-and-down, she exited the store without a purchase. Thumbing a message into her iPhone, she texted Blonde.

TEXT MESSAGES:

EVETTE TO BLONDE: Got that nigga! I'm 'bout tah get'cha money!"

Seeing Grinch come out of the store, she tucked her phone into her True jeans, and walked up to Grinch, with her .380 drawn, "Where da fuck is Blonde's money, nigga!!"

"HM! !"

"POP!" As Evette was talking, Grinch, threw his bag into her face, causing a small distraction. His quick reaction only made Evette pop a shot off. Nearly shooting Grinch, Evette, was under attack. Outweighed, Grinch, over powered her, and took her gun from her, "BITCH, WHO DA FUCK..."

"UGGH. UGGGH!" The two of them tussled, but not for long, "MM...MM .MM! BITCH-DON'T-YOU-EV-ER ROLL UP ON ME!" Grinch said, pistol whipping Evette.

"STOP! YOU'RE GONNA KILL HER..."

"...OH MY GOD..."

Our Love Is A Life Sentence

"...SOMEBODY CALL 9-1-1!" People said, standing around in a small crowd around Grinch and Evette. Grinch struck Evette in the face, talking to her with every blow. Hearing somebody say that they were going to call the cops made Grinch stop.

"What da fuck you got fo' me?!" Grinch said, trying to stuff his huge hands in to Evette's tight True pockets. Pulling out a couple stacks, her iPhone, and a baggie of Khalifa.

Standing, Grinch, tucked Evette's strap in his waistband, and ran off with the rest of her belongings in his hand.

"Burrr-ing-ing-ing ... Burrr-ing-ing-ing...Yea!" Looking at the name Blonde on the LCD screen of Evette's iPhone, made Grinch answer it.

"Who's this?!" Blonde asked.

"It's Grinch, bitch! Oh, you wanna send ma'fuckas at me, huh?!"

"Where's 'Vette. What you doin' wit' her phone, Grinch?!"

"Dat bitch bloody as hell, and half dead! Fuckin' wit' me! And Bitch you ain't gettin' shit! You gon' fuck around an' get the same as her..."

...CLICK!

Blonde didn't want to hear any more.

"Fuck, 'Vette!" She said, dialing Dice's number.

"Oouu-ah... Daddy ... Eh, daddy. Yes, like that ... Put that dick on me like that!" Dice's girlfriend, Alex, wailed, as he gripped the love handles of her well-proportioned body, fucking her from the back. Alex was close to three hundred pounds, and Dice loved every bit of her. She was a goddess to him. She was there when no one else was. So, she had a special place in his heart.

"Nnn...Nnnnn ... Nnnn...Nnn..." Dice's phone was blowing up.

This was the fifth time it buzzed, "Shit! Let me see who the fuck keep blowin' me up," Dice said, pulling his dick out of Alex's sweet hole of pleasure.

Looking at Blonde and a few other people's names on his screen the missed calls made him nervous. A couple of people hitting his line never called him unless something was wrong, "Yo?!" He said, calling Blonde back.

"Meet me at West Side grocer. Grinch just pistol-whipped Evette, it's bad!"

"What?! What the fuck happened?!" Dice asked, yelling in to his cell phone.

"Just meet me ... Click!"

CHAPTER 6 OVER SPILLED BLOOD

Evette Renay Ford, was the middle child of three. As a child, her mother would often abandon her and her two brothers. Strung out on crack cocaine her mother would leave them a week or two at a time. Eventually, their mother's crack binges cost her the custody of them. They were split up, and shipped to different group homes until their mother could prove to the courts that she was drug free. Her mother's and she resented her mother for not being a loving, responsible parent.

"Bitch, you betta get out here and get ya own. I ain't got time to baby ya ass!" Her mother told her when she was twelve. By the time she was fourteen she was on the block serving rocks with

the other neighborhood drug dealers. She was even selling crack to her own mother. The mixture of her mother's cruel words, and the streets turned her into a street monster. By the time her mother had regained custody of the three siblings, it was too late. The streets had already taken a hold of them.

Our Love Is A Life Sentence

By the time Evette was twenty years old, she had been to three different group homes, had been sent to juvie multiple times, and to the County Jail once she turned eighteen. Her older brother, Vernon, was serving a life sentence for the murder of a childhood friend. During a dice game, he got heated during an argument about a twenty-dollar bet, pull out his strap, and shot his friend, dead. Her younger brother, Tyson, was a year and a half in on a 'five-to-ten-year state bid, and her mother was still strung out on crack. Thinking of them made her feel like she was left all alone to fend for herself, much like the way she felt when she was twelve years old.

Now at twenty-three years old she laid in the street half dead. Blood ran from her face, and left a puddle of crimson liquid beneath her head.

Word of her being pistol-whipped traveled fast. Her mother ran from a crack-house to see about her baby, Blonde, was pulling up, and Dice was on his way.

"Ma'am, do you know who did this to you," a police officer asked. as the EMT lifted her into the back of an ambulance. "Grinch did that to her," a bystander told the police. Barely conscious, Evette, didn't say a word. As her mother stepped aboard, the ambulance doors shut, and they were whisked away to the hospital.

Our Love Is A Life Sentence

Our Love Is A Life Sentence

AT (NEOCC), WHILE DIVA AND ROMAN ENJOYED THEIR VISIT, a jail-house mule named, Jarvis, was strip-searched, and lead to a small room where lawyers and their clients met.

"You're here," the guard told Jarvis, opening the conference room door open.

"Thanks," Jarvis said, walking into the room, and taking a seat at a table across from Samuel.

"How's it going?" Samuel asked Jarvis.

"It's goin'," Jarvis replied.

After small talk about his case, Jarvis went to the door, and peeped to see if there were any guards coming.

"We're cool," he told Samuel.

Quickly Samuel dumped his Legal materials onto the table, and removed the secret panel inside of his briefcase.

Digging the PK out of it, he placed it on the table, and as quickly as he removed

the panel he put it back in place. As he stuffed his legal document's back into his attaché, Jarvis, sat back down. Taking a finger, he wiped Vaseline from the back of his ear, and rubbed it into his palms. Then he lubricated the small pickle shaped package. Looking up at the door, he lifted himself from his chair with one hand, and-pushed the package up his rectum with his other. Standing, he clinched

81

Our Love Is A Life Sentence

his ass cheeks, and squatted to make sure that it was secure. While he was doing all of this, Samuel, stood guard at the door, "You finished?"

He asked Jarvis,

"Yea-yup," Jarvis said, sitting back down.

"I'll let the guard know that you're ready," Samuel said. Walking out of the conference room, he never looked back. The pay was the only thing he enjoyed out of the whole ordeal. Not the meeting to get the drugs, not the bubble-guts he got when he walked them in to the prison, and he didn't care for seeing a man stuff his ass with a package the size of a small dick.

"There go ya man," Roman said, watching Samuel walk through the visiting room to exit the prison. Without turning around, Diva, watched Samuel walk pass through the refection in the plexiglass that seperated her from her King. "He's ready to go ... Room #3... Okay, thank you," she listened as Samuel, and the guard talks before he handed Samuel back his identification.

"Guess eh'thang went well," Diva said.

"I guess ... Let me see them titties. Hurry up before the guard turn back around," Roman told Diva.

"Smack," Diva sucked her teeth, but did as her King told her. Digging her pink colored, manicured fingers in to her

82

button-up, she pulled out her breast, and exposed her nipple for a couple seconds.

"Fuck! I want you so baaad, bae!"

"I want you too, hubby," Diva said into the phone, low and seductively. Shifting his dick around in his loose, elastic pants, he tried to control himself.

"I wanna suck that dick till you squirt ya hot cum all down my throat," Diva said, then she bit her bottom lip, and her nose twitched as her upper lip quivered.

Seeing that the guard was preoccupied, Roman, took a rolled-up piece of tissue paper from his upper shirt pocket, and laid it on his left thigh.

"You know what I miss?" Diva asked as Roman pulled his dick out.

"I miss you fucking my tight, little ass, cummin' all inside of it. That cum be sooo haaawwwt!"

"You miss me fuckin' you in ya ass, huh?"

"Helllll yee-ah!"

"You bet' not give it to nobody," Roman said, jacking himself off, periodically, closing his eyes. Concentrating as he pictured the things Diva was saying in his head.

"I'm locking it all up until you get home, daddy."

"Ah ... Ahh. . .Mmmm, baby... Baby," Roman whispered in a light pant.

"Come on, daddy, cum for me," Diva said, licking her lips. Cum in my mouth," she continued, watching Roman's arm doing a jerking motion.

"Uggghh ... Ah. . .Mmm. . .Whhew. . . I'M CAH'MIN', BAE! I'm cummin!!! ," Jerking his dick, he pumped his ass as if he was fucking his Queen. Releasing himself, she shot hot cum unto the tissue that sat on his lap.

"You feel betta," Diva asked.

"Hell yea. I need that," Roman said, watching the guard as he wiped himself off.

"We got ten minutes," Diva told Roman how much time they had left on their visit. It took her a couple hours to get there, but visits were only for an hour. She hated that shit, and so did Roman. She inquired, "How long are our visits goin' to be when you get to where ya going?"

"Like six to eight hours, I think," Roman said.

"That's wassup. I need ah eight-hour visit, so this shit like ah job ... Ha ha ha," Diva said, jokingly.

"Ha ha ha...Hell yea ... Hey, did you check on that spot for the rental car shit?" Roman asked Diva about a small parking lot he was trying to buy.

"I called. I'm waiting for ah call back. You really try'na open up ah rental car spot, huh, hubby?"

"Yea, we gotta do something' wit' the money we makin'. Clean that shit up, you know?"

"Damn hubby, it's time to go," Diva said, checking her gold Rolex timepiece.

"Yea, the guard's walkin' ova now. Go 'head, bae. I don't want him tellin' you, you gotta leave," Roman said.

"Okay. Love you, hubby."

"Love you, too, wifey." "You callin' me, later?"

"Yea, I'ma call 'round eight."

'Wight," Diva said, blowing Roman a kiss. He caught it, and placed it on his chest.

WHILE DIVA AND ROMAN WERE ON THEIR VISIT, Evette was getting stitched up at Ohio Valley Hospital. Grinch had blacked both of her eyes, split her head opened from her forehead through her eyebrow, busted her lip, and knocked her two front teeth out. Blonde cried looking at her. Tears flooded from the rims of her eyes, but they weren't tears of sadness, they were tears of anger. Evette's mother, Mona, called for a ride. After seeing her daughter, she went looking for the bastard that had done such a thing to her baby. Dice called around trying to locate Grinch, but was unsuccessful. Finally, fresh off her visit, Diva, answered her phone, "Wassup, brother?" She said into her cellphone.

"Sis, what da fuck is Ew-Wee's number?!" Dice asked with his voice full of anger and frustration.

"Oh, hol' up. What's wrong?!" Diva asked.

"Dat ma'fucka Grinch fucked Evette up. Busted her shit all up. She got stitches all in her shit, black eyes, her fuckin' front teeth all knocked da fuck out!" Dice said, hysterically, walking with

Blonde and Evette out of the hospital.

 "Whhhaaat?!! Dat nigga crazy!"

"Oh, he ain't seen crazy, yet! I'ma handled that nigga fo' dis shit. That's my word!"

"Here you go," Diva said about to read Ew-wee's number off, "You got something to write with?" She asked.

"Nah, I can remember it," Dice said. "A'ight. 8-1-2-3-4-4-0...72-4-8-1-2-3-4-4-0.'

"Cool, let me call dis nigga. Where you at sis?"

"On my way back. I'll be back in the 'Burgh in about an hour. I'll meet: up with y'all when I get there."

'Wight, love you."

"Love you, too, Dice. Be careful."

"I got dis, sis'," Dice assured Diva.

"I need to get my car," Evette said, as she got into Dice's car.

"I gotta get mines, too," Blonde said. She had rode to the hospital with Dice, and left her car parked behind Divas. Everything north of Evette's shoulders hurt. Her head throbbed, it felt like it was about to explode. Her right eye was shut, and the other swollen. Her tongue fiddled around where her two front teeth used to be. She was in bad shape.

"Hey 'Vette, we gon' get'cha car, and I'ma leave my truck there. You're in no condition to be driving," Dice said, dialing Ew-Wee's number.

"I want you to stay at the transport spot for a couple days till I sort this shit out. We'll get'cha medication on the way there," Dice said, in between punching Ew-Wee's number into his cellphone, "Beep-beep-beep.... Beep-beep-beep-beep," they all could hear the numbers being punched into the phone's keypad.

After a few rings, Ew-Wee answered, "Yea, who dis?!"

"This Dice, yo! What's Grinch's number? I need to holla at ol' boy," Dice said, with an aggressive tone of voice.

"I don't know. He just gotta new phone. I'm waitin' fo' him to call, and hit me wit' da number. Why tho, wassup?"

"Fam', dat nigga did some wild shit to my people. Tell dat nigga he got 'til seven to call me, or it's gon' be some mo' blood spilled, fo' real! CLICK!"

"Dice? Bro, calm down." Ew-Wee was saying, until he realized that Dice had banged on him. "Grinch, man, what da fuck! You got dis nigga Dice try'na get at you now. I'm not gettin' caught up in ya shit, gee. I'm tellin' you dat now!" Ew-Wee told Grinch.

CHAPTER 7 CHOICES

AT (NEOCC), AFTER ROMAN'S VISIT, he moved Smooth in to his cell. While they were doing that, his jailhouse mule placed a sheet over his cell door window for privacy. Pulling his pants and boxer's down, he squatted over the toilet, and grunted a few times, "UUUGGGH ...AH, UGGGH ... AH, UUUGGHHH!"

SPLASH!

Using his abdominal muscles, he pushed the package out of his ass. It plopped inside of the toilet. Using a pair of blue surgical gloves he removed the package from the bowel of the toilet and threw it in to the sink. After wiping his ass, he pressed the sink button.

CLUNK, SWOOOSSSH...CLUNK, SWOOOSH.

It sounded as it released hot water in to the stainless-steel sink. Taking a small bottle of shampoo off the sink, he popped its lid open, and poured its thick liquid all over the balloon-wrapped package. Cleaning it of any fecal matter, he took a razor and cut the knot off the balloon to expose the drugs inside of it.

"Hmph, dat's what I'm talkin' 'bout," the mule said, pulling the Ziploc bag of drugs out of the balloon.

Thoroughly lathering it up, he cleansed it. Making sure all his fecal matter was cleaned off it.

Walking down the upper tier, Roman, looked to see if the Unit C.O. was watching him, and he wasn't paying him any attention. His face was buried in to the Sports Section of the USA Today newspaper. So Roman made his way to his mule's partially parted, sheet-covered, cell door. "Knock, knock!" He knocked on the door.

"Yo?!" Roman heard his mule call out.

"It's me, fam'," Roman responded.

"Come on, bro," the mule said, telling Roman he could enter his cell.

Roman checked for the guard again, and he was still reading his newspaper. Slipping in to the cell, Roman, made sure that the sheet did not fall from the cell door, "We good?" He asked his mule.

"Most def', we great!" The mule Said as Roman watched him dry off the PK with a towel. Opening the towel, he gave Roman a look at his package.

"You ready to crack it," the mule asked.

"Yea. Hell yea. Nigga's try'na cop ASAP. Plus, I know y'all try'na smoke ah lil some'in'," Roman said. He was feeling good about himself, his visit, and his mule successfully getting his drugs in to the high security facility.

"You think we should smoke this early. You know that C.O. be walking, checking cells, an' shit," the mule reminded Roman of the C.O.'s knack of being a nuisance. He may have been pre-occupied with reading the newspaper at that time, but his normal. routine consisted of him walking the unit the top of every hour, and checking cells. The inmates had a certain call they would use to alert eachother when he was on the prowl, but that call wouldn't save them if he smelled weed coming from their cell. So, at that moment, Roman, was not thinking wisely. The mule reminded him of that. "Yea, you right. It'll be gravy tonight," Roman said, with

a change of mind.

"Yea. Our regular will be on tonight. You know he laid back. He doesn't give ah fuck," the mule continued to say.

"You right. But bag half of dat shit up, tho 'cause after four o'clock count, we rollin'. I'ma get dat shit gone during chow, you know?"

"Got you, bro."

"Bet. Get it done."

"Might, tell my celly to come up. We gon' knock this shit out really quick," the mule said, cutting the knot off the balloon with a razor he spits from his mouth.

'Got'cha. Check to see if the guard's watchin'," Roman said to the mule.

Stepping out of the cell, the mule looked down at the C.O. in the bubble and he was still reading the paper, "Come on, bro," he told Roman.

Roman slid out of the cell right behind him. Looking down in to the rec area, the mule's celly and Roman made eye contact.

Roman nodded at him, and the mule's celly knew that it was time to bag-up the product.

Inside of his cell, Roman's new celly, Smooth, laid on the top bunk reading one of Roman's Hip Hop Weekly's.

"Yo, fam', I got three bins full of commissary. You're welcome to whatever you want. Don't even ask. Just get whatever you need. I got hygiene shit, whatever. Aaannd tonight I'ma have some'in' fo' you to smoke. You smoke, right?"

"You know it!" Smooth said, sitting up. Wondering how Roman got drugs in to the jail. He knew Roman had gone on a visit, but he also knew that the jail didn't have any

Our Love Is A Life Sentence

contact visits. So how Roman did it remained a mystery to him.

"So yo, you find out when you goin' down fo' ya' detention hearing?" Roman asked, standing at the front of their bunks.

"Yea, my people said that the lawyer called, and told them that I'll be goin' down next week. But my homie is goin' down in a couple days. He said he got a slim chance of goin' home, 'cause

he's the head of the indictment, like you said," Smooth told Roman.

"Tol' y'all. What'cha lawyer say?"

"He said he gon' do what he can. He said I gotta fifty-fifty percent chance, 'cause of my pending case, you know?"

"Yea, like I was sayin'."

"You were on point, big homie."

"Pam, I know these ma'fuckas."

"Man bro, I'm try'na get outta dis bitch"

"See, what they doin' is try'na stall ah nigga out. Make y'all sit around and think about y'all freedom," Roman explained, taking a seat on his bottom bunk.

"They want y'all to snitch, an' shit," Roman said, looking up at the bottom -of the top bunk. He wanting to hear Smooth's response. He was still try'na fill him out. He knew not to say too much to him about anything that he could use to lighten his sentence.

"Dat ain't gon' happen" They already tried dat shit," Smooth said, looking at an article in the Hip Hop Weekly, but his mind wasn't registering one word written on the page in the magazine.

"Oh yea," Roman acted like he didn't know that already.

"Yea. When they ran up in my shit, they were like, one or-two things can happen; you can work with us and stay out or go to prison. Man, I passed up on dat shit! I told dem ma'fuckas handcuff me! So, did my man Banks. They went at him wit' the same shit," Smooth told Roman.

"So, you know eh'body ... Well, most of ya co-dees that went home are workin' wit' dem people," Roman gave Smooth the real.

"Hmph! .1 was thinkin' dat shit. Dat shit's crazy!" Smooth said, shaking his head.

"Fo' real, tho ... If you got any paper out there I would hire a lawyer' fo' ya detention hearing', 'cause they gon' give you ah plant. The lawyer they give you is going to be workin' for the DA," Roman sat back on the bottom bunk, and told Smooth.

"Man, they hit me. Took all my paper. I gotta couple dollars on the streets, but not dat much. How much ah

Our Love Is A Life Sentence

lawyer gon' cost me fo' the hearing'," Smooth asked, looking down at the bottom bunk. Looking at Roman's fresh white Al's hanging from his bunk.

"Like five-to-seven gee's," Roman told Smooth.

"Shit, I ain't got dat," Smooth said, sitting back on his bunk. Roman had it to give, but he didn't know Smooth like that. He felt sorry for the young hustler, but his problem wasn't his. He went through the motion, now it was their turn to do the same.

"Damn!" Roman said.

Deep inside he knew the only way for the duo, Banks and Smooth, to get out was to cooperate. They didn't have a chance with a court appointed attorney. Smooth had mentioned that the Feds offered them an opportunity to stay out on the streets, and they both declined. Which meant they may have missed their only opportunity to use their get out of jail free card. Because by the time they made it to their Detention Hearing, their co-dees would have provided the Feds with enough information about them that would turn the stay an extended one.

"Hopefully, you'll be a'ight. Hey yo, tho'..." Roman said, slamming his fist in to his hand, "When we come in tonight I'ma go over my 'Busted By The Feds' book with you. Matter of fact, after we run through it, you can have that joint. Y'all gon' need dat ma'fucka. And I'ma give you some pointers on what to tell ya lawyer to say at ya Detention Hearing," Roman said.

"Good look, big homie. Hey tho', not to be all in ya business, but how much time they give you?" As Smooth was making this statement, Roman thought he was going to ask about how he got the drugs in to the jail, but he didn't.

"They hit me wit' ten," Roman told the young hustler.

"DAAAAMMMN! Fo' how much shit, big homie?!"

"Five ki's are more of coc'. They gave me five years, but the 851'd me, and made it ten," Roman educated Smooth a little bit on how the Feds worked.

"Damn homie, that's crazy. I think that's what they got on us. I think that's what my lawyer told me in the courtroom," Smooth said, shaking his head.

"Yea. Come on, homie. Let's get the fuck outta dis cell fo' ah minute. You play Bones?" Roman asked Smooth if he played dominoes.

"Yea but I wanna call my people, see if my lawyer called back," Smooth said, climbing down off the top bunk.

"Yea, see what's up," Roman said as the left their cell. Looking down at the inmates in the rec area, Smooth noticed that a phone was open, and Roman observed the domino table, "WHO GOT NEXT?" Roman called out.

Our Love Is A Life Sentence

"You homie," One of the domino players called out. Shortly after four O'clock count, chow was called, and all the inmates on the unit, scurried out of the unit entrance. The cafeteria was down the hall. Inmates from different units ate together. Roman told Smooth that he would be able to see his homie Banks at the chow hall.

"See what unit he on, "I'll send him a lil care-package," Roman told Smooth.

Coming out of C-Unit which was across from B-Unit, Banks spotted Smooth, "Bro Bro," he called out.

"Wassup, fam'. How's dat shit over there?" Smooth asked Banks. "Shit a'ight. We gotta couple homies over there. They looked out," Banks said as they walked down the hallway to the chow hail.

"What up, boy. You good ova there. I gotta lil care package for you. When we come back slow up a lil, and I'll grab it fo' you," Roman told banks with a hand shake,

"Good lookin'," said Banks.

"No doubt, fam'," Roman said. picking up his pace, he let the two young boys catch up, and conducted business. He and a couple of his homies passed little packages of drugs to other inmates that travel the hallway to, the chow hail. Smooth never saw a thing. He was clueless about how things were run in the prison, and Roman was planning on

97

Our Love Is A Life Sentence

keeping him blind to certain details of about his jailhouse operations.

"So, when they got you goin' down?" Banks asked Smooth.

"Next week," Smooth said as they waited to enter the chow hall.

"I go down in a couple days. I need up out dis bitch," Banks said, entering the chow hall.

Shit me too," Smooth said as they looked around the huge dining room. "Damn, dis shit's big," He continued.

Checking faces at tables and in line they recognized a lot of their Pittsburgh homies.

"Damn, these ma'fuckas got the whole city locked up," He said, shaking

his head.

CHAPTER 8 SHIT'S GETTIN' REAL

Compared to the real killers in the 'hood, Grinch, wasn't really a tough guy. No one never heard of him busting his gun. he got money back in the day, but never ran things. He was just a part of a crew that got money, and he got indicted back in 2003 with the rest of them.

Most people remembered him by the Maroon colored Benz, sitting on Lorinsers, he had. Every since his release in 2011, he had caught bad breaks. After only being home for a month he got sent back to Federal prison for a year because of a violation. When he got out the second time, he worked for a while, but seeing all his homies getting money made him want to try his hand in the game one last time. Having had given work to Ew-Wee back in the day, he felt it only right that Ew-Wee looked out for him, and Ew-Wee agreed, and fronted him a couple pounds of Granddaddy Purple. But weed money wasn't the kind of money that Grinch was trying to make. All the truly paid homies were serving bags, "H", that dog food, also known as heroin. Like many others, he heard that you could get rich over night off selling bags, and that's what he needed, a really quick lick. He wasn't trying to stay in the game for long, he wanted to make just enough to take care of his two kids, and start a small business. Looking for a bag connect, Blonde's name kept coming up. So, when he finally came across her at a local bar, he asked her about copping some work off her. Not really knowing him, but being she had heard about his money-making days, she took a chance, and decided to give him a shot.

Taking the flip money, he owed Ew-Wee, Grinch, copped fifty bricks of dope for $12,500. He gave her $7,000 of Ew-Wee's money up front, paid her two stacks a couple days later, and still owed her a few stacks. But once Ew-Wee heard about him using his money to flip bags, he got the ten stacks Grinch owed him, and cut his weed supply off. This left him unable to pay Blonde the rest of the money he owed her. unable to do so he started avoiding her, and that's what lead to the beef they were having.

"Where's my phone and my money?" Evette asked, looking over the contents giving to her upon, her release from the hospital. The only things sealed in the plastic hospital bag was her ID and her keys.

"It ain't in there?!" Dice looked over at Evette, and asked.

"They must have taken it. I had a couple stacks on me. Turn around. I want my shit!" Evette barely mumbled.

"Nah sis', that nigga must've taken ya shit!" Blonde said. The car got quiet. They all thought about what Grinch did to Evette, but neither of them said a word about it. A silence set in the atmosphere for several seconds.

"Oh shit! you know what, sis'?!" Blonde said, breaking the eerie silence.

"WHAT, SIS'?!" Evette asked, barely able to turn around, and look at Blonde.

"We can find out exactly where Grinch is at. You got that phone tracker on ya shit," Blonde reminded Evette.

"Ew shit! Hell yea!" Dice looked at Blonde through his rearview mirror with a smile on his face.

"Let's go get dat nigga!" Evette said, in pain, but ready to take out the man that was causing her so much pain.

"Nah, you need to rest, 'Vett. Let us handle dis fo' you," Dice said.

"I ain't wit' it! Look at what that nigga did to me, Dice."

"I'ma kill dat nigga!" Evette said, holding her head, with excruciating pain surging through her thick skull.

"No! Look, this is what where gon' do," Dice said.

APPROXIMATELY, AN HOUR AND A HALF LATER, Grinch, was still over Ew-Wee's house. Ew-Wee wanted Grinch out of his spot, but didn't have the heart to make his big homie leave. Besides that, he didn't want to seem like a bitch. As he weighed up ounce after ounce of Khalifa Kush, Grinch rolled up blunts for them to smoke.
"So how much you get off dat bitch?!" Ew-Wee asked.
"Ah couple racks, ah strap, and dis iPhone," Grinch told his friend. "Ya ass came up, ha ha ha," Ew-Wee said, with a chuckle.
"Ah lil some'in', some'in', ha ha ha," Grinch, jokingly, agreed.

The hour that Dice warned them about had come and gone without incident. At first, while they waited for the end of the hour: to come to its end, they were on point. Expecting something to happen. At least another call from Dice, but that never happened. Ew-Wee even thought about moving his product from his spot. That was his first mind, but he second guessed his way of thinking. "That nigga, Dice, is just mad. He'll calm down," he told Grinch.
"Yea, whateva," Grinch replied, not knowing how much damage he had done to Evette's face. If he did, he would've realized how sever the problem was.

"We need to call some bitches ova; bro. I got a couple dollars, ah new strap, I'm feelin' good!"

"Ha ha ha. Nigga, you crazy. Let me finish weighin' dis shit up. Then we can put some in' together," Ew-Wee said, dropping what he thought was an ounce on the circular base of the digital scale. "It shouldn't take that much longer," He continued to say, looking at the three out of ten pounds he had left to bag up.

"I mind as well make the call now. You know it takes them hoes ah couple hours to get ready, find babysitter's, an' shit."

'Aight. Go 'head. Hey yo?! You try'na step out fo' ah minute, hit da club's up? I know ya situation, but..."

"Situation?! Maaan, ain't no situation. I'm not worried 'bout no nigga, and I'm definitely not worried 'bout no bitches. Unless, they try'na flick, straight up! Hey tho, fam', let me give you ah stack on ah couple of them pee's," Grinch said, trying to make away to flip the money he took off Evette.

"Oh, now you wanna get back in to the weed game? You funny as hell, yo!"

"Come on wit' da bullshit, Wee!"

"Ha ha ha ... I 'on't know, nigga. You like to take a nigga's money, and flip dat shit elsewhere," Ew-Wee reminded Grinch of the underhanded shit he did to him.

"Stop dat, yo!"

"Nab, fo' real, you can't be doin' dat shit with my loot. If you try'na be in da dope game do it wit'cha own paper. Look at what doin' dat shit got you in to," Ew-Wee said, tying a knot in to the end of a baggie full of KK.

"I got you, fam'. Say no mo'," Grinch agreed to Ew-Wee's terms. "Go 'head, take two of dem 015L" Ew-Wee said, looking over at the pounds, sitting in two garbage bags on the living room floor.

NNNN ... NNN. . .NNNN..

Evette's iPhone vibrated in Grinch's hand. Grind pressed end, and stopped the vibrations. Then he dialed one of his girl's numbers to set up a hook up for him and his man.

Our Love Is A Life Sentence

AN HOUR LATER, while Grinch and Ew-Wee waited for their lady friends to arrive at Ew-Wee's spot, Evette, was pulling up to Ohio Valley Hospital. And at the same time that she was pulling up to Ohio Valley Hospital, Blonde and Dice were pulling up down the block from Ew-Wee's spot. Evette's iPhone was tracked to the street Ew-Wee lived on.

Seeing Evette walking up to the receptionist desk in her condition made the nurse at the desk cringe, "What in the hell happened to her?" She thought, "May I help you?" She asked Evette.

"Yea, I was here earlier, and my cellphone and money is missin' from my property," Evette told the nurse that could not keep her eyes off of her battered and bruised face.

"Ok, let me make a couple calls, and find out who exactly handled your property," the nurse said as Blonde pulled her black hoodie over her head, and clinched her Glock 17 with her glove-covered hand.

"You want me to do this?" Dice asked Blonde.

"Nah Dice. I got this. All this is about the money he owes me, Blonde said, about to open the car door.

"You know it's at least to niggas in there."

"Yea, I know. I can handle this, tho."

"I'll be here waitin'," Dice said, killing the car's engine.

105

He couldn't turn the car's lights out without killing the ignition.

Blonde got out of the car, walked to Ew-Wee's front door, and knocked on it lightly. She didn't want to startle whoever was inside.

INSIDE OF EW-WEE'S SPOT, "Bout time. These bitches are finally here. Get dat; I'ma use the bathroom, bro," Grinch said.

"You still ain't give me dat stack neither, nigga. When you come out dat bitch I want my money," Ew-Wee said, walking in front of Grinch to open the door for who they thought was their date's. In order to get to the bathroom, Grinch, had to get pass Ew-Wee, and go up the steps. The bathroom was upstairs. "Come on, nigga! You movin' all slow, an' shit. I gotta piss like ah ma'fucka!" Grinch said, brushing pass Ew-Wee. "I got you tho, soon as I get out da bathroom. "You lucky I don't do you like I did dat bitch, and take all ya shit, nigga," Grinch thought, climbing the third step.

On the opposite side of Ew-Wee's door, Blonde, could hear the voice of the goon that hurt her sister, and best friend. The lame that owed her a few stacks. But she no longer wanted the-money, she was out for revenge. Hearing the door unlocking, she pulled the drawstring on her hoodie, causing it to draw close around
her face. Then the front door open, and what Ew-Wee saw was a surprise, "PLOW! PLOW!" One shot entered his throat, shattered his Adam's apple, and exiting out the right side of his neck. Blonde stood over him to deliver her

second, and fatal shot. Standing directly of Ew-Wee she put one right in the center of his head.

The first shot made Grinch, jump, and see what exactly had happened. Catching Ew-Wee's body fallin, and blood shooting out of his neck, made him climb the steps faster. The .380 he had taken off Evette was on the couch in the living room along with the two pounds he got off Ew-Wee. Seeing the petite hooded assassin made these things to decamp from his mind.

POP-POP-POP-POP-POP!

 Seeing Grinch trying to get away made Blonde squeeze her trigger, but known of the shots seemed to hit him.

Stepping inside of the apartment, Blonde, carefully looked side-to-side, and then quickly stepped closer towards the living room. The smell of weed got stronger and stronger, "Where is it?" she asked herself under her breath. "There it is," she said, seeing Grinch's two pounds on the couch. Hearing someone's feet pitter-patter across the roof, she assumed it was Grinch escaping

out of a back window. "'Vette's gat," she said, recognizing Evette's .380. Then she looked around for something to put the two pounds

in, and the living room closet caught her eye. Getting closer to it, the stronger the scent of Exotic Buds got. When she

pulled back the metal closet door, it squeaked, and gave a little resistance. But she forced it to draw back on its metal track, "DAMN!" She said, seeing the two garbage bags of KK. Throwing the two pounds in to one of the bags, she stuck her strap in to
her waistband opposite of Evette's and grabbed up the bags of bud.
Hiding in the backyard, Grinch's adrenaline was pumping through his veins. His whole body was overcome with fear. He thought he just saw his friend get killed, and his thoughts were correct. Ew-Wee was dead and stinking. He knew that the killer would leave the spot shortly after the shots stopped. So, he hid in the abyss of the night until he heard his friend's killer leave from the premises, and then he saw a shadowy figure run pass the driveway that seperated Ew-Wee's place from his neighbor's, with what he believed was the two bags of weed.
Moving without any more hesitation, he went to the back patio, and shattered it. He had to make sure his friend was dead, and didn't need assistance. At least that's what he told himself.
All he really wanted was the for bundles of cash he saw Ew-Wee stuffed in to the refrigerator freezer, and whatever weed that was left. But he knew he had to be fast, so he

darted through the spot. There he was. Grinch, held his hand to his mouth, and then,

"BLLLAAAAH. BLAH!" Grinch threw his insides up. He had never seen the inside of anyone's brains blown out. Seeing the sight of the carnage made out of his homies had made him spit up. Stepping over him, he went in to the freezer, and grabbed the four five-thousand dollar stacks his late friend stashed inside of it. Then without looking down at his friend turned gunshot victim, he stepped over his dead body, and escaped into the night.

Three minutes from the murder scene, Dice, pulled in to a back alley. "Here, give dat to 'Vette," Dice said. Opening the glove compartment, he handed Blonde a burn out phone, and then he pressed a button to pop the trunk. Then he grabbed the two garbage bags of weed, and threw them in to the boot of his girl's Charcoal colored Malibu LT. After closing the trunk, he tore off a special piece of reflector tape from the license plate. He had got it from a spy-store. The tape prevented onlookers from getting a clear view of his license plate number.

"Take off ya hoodie, babe," he said to Blonde as he pulled off. "You get him," he then asked.

"I think! I got Ew-Wee, tho," Blonde said, taking a deep breath. She was sure that the weed-man was dead.

"Ew-Wee?!" Dice said, surprised by her answer.

"Yea! He came to the door so I shot him. Then I shot at Grinch's ass, he was running up the steps. I don't know if I hit him, tho. I might of, I'm not sure." Everything that happened replayed in Blonde's
head as she explained the events to Dice.

"Hmph! You did good, babe. Now, they'll all know we're not to be fucked wit'! Give me ah kiss," Dice said.

"Mmmmuuu-ah," Blonde kissed her street od, not feeling any remorse for killing the innocent man that supplied the 'hood with Exotic Weed.

Sophia "Blonde" McCormick was a crazy mix of Irish and Sicilian, which explained her craziness and olive oil skin. She was 5'8" with hazel eyes and long lashes that any woman would kill for. Her dirty blonde hair was a river of tresses that streamed down her back, and fell several inches from her voluptuous buttocks. Her hair was naturally jet black, but ever since her youth she had dyed it blonde. Growing up she never r ally knew her father. He was constantly on tours with the military. Besides that, he really didn't care for her mother, and didn't want anything to do with her. When she was ten her father married, a d had two children, and he cared for them more then he cared for her. To date, she could only recall meeting her siblings twice.

Our Love Is A Life Sentence

Her calls to her father normally went unanswered, so often cried herself to sleep and lashed out violently because of the unwanted way her makers made her feel. Her mother was a College graduate that traded a good job in for a crack pipe, and street career as a crack whore, that exchanged her body for small pieces of crack. She was a decent, woman whenever she was clean of drugs. Which was always during her short stays at the Allegheny County Jail. That: was the only time Blonde could sit and talk to her mother sober. Whenever she was on t e streets her addiction made her hard to keep up with. Whenever Blonde got old enough she would chase her mother
in and out of crack houses, pleading and begging her to stop using.

Her mother's choice to choose drugs over her made her angry, and eventually made her grandparent's take custody of her when she was seven years old.

Raised in Sheridan, a pre-dominantly white section that was overrun with blacks in the mid-eighties, she had no other choice but to befriend them and learn their culture. By the time she went to live with her grandparent's in the late nineties, Greenway Middle School and Langley High School was occupied by 'eighty percent African American students. So, most of her friends were black. So, it was nothing for her to pick up on the slang and other ways of the streets. Her first boyfriend was a bailer named Dom P. He was killed during a robbery when she was seventeen. He taught her how to get money, and while doing so he turned her on to popping pills and smoking weed. When he got killed she was left with a few bands and fifteen bricks of dope that was worth thirty-six hundred dollars, and a Seven Series BMW with a six hundred dollar a month car note.

Riding with Dice on the way to the transport spot, she thought about all of this. Then she thought about how Ew-Wee's head exploded when her bullet hit and imploded his skull. Sending bone fragments and blood splatter throughout the front entrance of his home. Then she thought about Grinch fleeing up the steps. She wondered if one of her bullets hit him.

"Nn ... Nnnn ... Nn," Dice's cellphone vibrated, and lit up in his lap as he was driving. He checked the caller on the ID, pressed send, and answered it, "Wassup Sis'?" Dice asked, looking over at Blonde as she stared out of the passenger side window.

"Where you at," Diva asked Dice.

"On the way to my spot. Why, wassup, sis'?"

Our Love Is A Life Sentence

"I've been try'na get at Ew-wee, he ain't answerin'. .1 need some'in' to smoke. Did you cop anything from him, yet?"

"Yea, earlier. I got Some'in' nice fo' you. I'll bring it over after I drop Blonde off," Dice said.

"Okay. Thank you, brother."

"No doubt," Dice said, hanging up, and sitting his cellphone back on his lap. "You a'ight?" Dice asked Blonde, placing his hand on her leg.

"Yea. I'm good, bae," Blonde replied, placing her hand over his. "You did ya thing," Dice said, looking over at her, and then back on the road.

"Nn ... Nnnn ... Nn," Dice's cellphone vibrated again, looking at Diva's number flashing on the screen he answered. He figured she forgot to give him a message from Roman. "Wassup, sis'?"

"They just found Ew-Wee dead. They said some bitches found him wit' his shit blown back. No wonder dat nigga wasn't answering his phone!" Diva informed Dice of the information he already knew.

"You bullshittin'! Hey Bee, somebody killed dat nigga, Ew-Wee!" Dice put on a front.

"Nah, fo' real?!" Blonde played along.

"Man, dat shit's crazy, sis'!" Dice acted as if he was devastated by what Diva told him. She didn't know

114

anything about the words Dice and Ew-Wee had, or his plan for handling the beef with Grinch, and he would keep it that way.

"Mm mm mm! Good thing you got to cop before dat nigga got smoked," Diva stated, not really caring about Ew-Wee. She just wanted to get high. "How long are you gon' be, bro?" She asked.

"'Bout an' hour or so," Dice told her.

"Shiiit! I'm on my way to meet ya as. I'm try'na smoke," Diva told Dice.

"A'ight, we pullin' up," Dice told her.

"How's 'Vette?"

"She's fucked up, Sis'. I ain't gon' lie,"

"Mm mm mm, I'm on my way."

CHAPTER 9 TELEPHONE LOVERS

Just as Diva was ready to exit her house, and head over to Dice's spot, her cellphone rung.

BLLLINGGG-AH.... BLLLINNGGG-AH...

Looking at the screen of her phone, she smiled when she saw that the incoming call was a private one from Youngstown, Ohio. "YOOOO?!"She answered.

"YOOOO?!" *Ha ha ha.* Roman said with a chuckle. He laughed when Diva hit him with his own greeting. She always knew how to put him in good spirits. She made him feel free. No bars, wires or prison could strip him of the freedom her love provided. "Wassup wit' you, wifey?"

"Nothin'. I was just about to go ova bro's spot," Diva never preferred to Dice by his name over the prison phone. Roman told her to always take extra precaution when talking about certain

"Okay. Did you enjoy ya visit?" Diva asked Roman.

"Always do. Even though I have to glare at ya beauty through scarred plexiglass.

"Aw, baby," Roman's words made Diva fall back on her bed in bliss. She missed her man so much. "Well, hopefully, I'll be able to hug and kiss you when they move you. How long you think it will take before they do?" Diva added.

"I can't wait to get outta here. I'm ready to start biddin'. But ah, my celly left today..."

"He did?!,"

"...Yea. I forgot to tell you. He rolled out early this mornin'. But yo! It took him like two weeks. So, I'm thinkin' like ah couple weeks," Roman said.

"Will I be able to bring you clothes and food?"

"Ha ha ha, nah, bae, ha ha ... It ain't gon' be dat sweet," Diva wanted to make sure her man had whatever luxury he could have. She wanted him to have an easy stay. "Shit! I ain't know. You know I'm new to this shit," Diva said, laying with her eyes closed.

"I know you didn't, wifey. But I will be able to touch you, and kiss you, you know?" Roman reminded Diva.

"Mmmm," Diva moaned as she rubbed her breast at the thought of Roman's touch. She needed him. She needed some dick. She wished he could fuck her then. "I can't wait fo' you to touch me," she said.

Hearing Diva say those words made Roman get quiet as his Dick stiffened.

Our Love Is A Life Sentence

"Oh yea?" He finally responded. Now as Diva rubbed herself, her pussy moistened, and soaked her panty lining. As an unrepentant ass man, Roman, thought about Diva's heart-shaped derrieres in the doggy-style position. One ass cheek tatted "All," and the other "Roman's." Diva had other tattoes but this one was special to Roman. Fucking her from the back he was always reminded of who's pussy her's was. It was all his. He fantasized about his thumbs separating the honey-colored mounds of her fat ass. Him pounding her jiggling glutes with his meaty, throbbing, slab of pussy-stuffer, and her thrusting her wet cock swallowing cunt back and-forth on his pleasure pole. Thinking these things made Roman grab a handful of his dick, and ask, "Is dat pussy wet?"

"You know it is. Your voice keeps it that way, daddy," Diva said, sliding her fifteen-hundred dollar Balmain jeans down, over her fat ass. Down to her panties, she got up from the bed, and went to her bedroom dresser to grab her Bedroom Kandi toy. Then she laid back on her bed, "Is dat dick hard, daddy?" She asked Roman. "FUCK YEA!" At that moment, Roman, believed that his dick was the hardest it had ever been. Then he thought of Diva's slender, tatted, 5'10" frame, slim waist, busty, firm tits, and darting nipples, her almond brown eyes and plump lips.

"Hmph!" Roman grunted.

"What?!" Diva asked rubbing her cut in a circular motion with her middle fingers. She wanted Roman to start talking dirty to her. He ever-ready pussy was gearing to explode.

"You know what I wanna do?" Roman asked.

"What, daddy?" Diva asked as she watched her hand run circles around her cut, inside of her lace panties.

"I wanna squeeze those pretty tits of yours, together, and run the tip of my tongue over your nipples. Then take each one of them into my mouth. Suck on them, and swirl my tongue around the areola."

"Then what, daddy?" Diva asked as she panted, taking deeper and deeper breathes.

"Kiss up your neck as I slip a couple of my fingers in and out of the wet hole between your legs, and get that pussy ready fo'

dis dick," Roman said, looking around the Unit at the other inmates and convicts. He made sure that he wasn't being too loud. Diva had momentarily made him forget where he was.

"Them I'ma kiss down ya neck, through ya tits, and down ya stomach..."

"Mmm ... Mm ... Mmmm hm," Diva moaned.

"...Put them legs on my shoulders, and kiss dat pussy through dem sexy lace panties you always wear. Pull dem to the side, and stick my tongue in and out of it." Roman explained in great detail.

"Eat dat pussy, daddy," Diva said, moaning seductively.

"VRRRRRNNNNNN..." Diva turned on her vibrator. What's dat?" Roman, asked dumbfounded.

My toy," Diva said, pulling her panties to the side of her clean-shaven beaver, and sliding her Bedroom Kandi toy into her pussy, "Mmmmmm..." She moaned in ecstasy.

"Fuck dat pussy fo' daddy. Make it cum," Roman instructed. He imagined the curvy, pink, dick-shaped vibrator entering the slit of Diva's pleasure-puffed cunt, and gripped hard on his man-piece again. This time he could feel the sticky precum that seeped through his thin, blue khaki jailhouse pants.

"You have two minutes left," The automatic voice recording reminded the couple.

"Shhh...Shut...Shut up, bitch!" Diva groaned.

"Come on, cum, baby," Roman said. Knowing that they were running out of time.

"VRRRR...NNNN...VRRRR...NNNN...UH-Oh...UGH...OOOH, Roman... Roman ... Roman..." As Diva fuck herself good with the vibrator, Roman, could her the toy going in-and-out of her pussy. Then she squirted all over her bedspread, "AAAAGGGH...Bay...Bay ... Bay-beee, I'm cummin'," She wailed.

"You cummin'?" Roman asked.

"Mm hm, yes!" Diva answered. "Love you, wifey," Roman said.

...CLICK!

The calling card had run out of minutes. Standing there for a few seconds, Roman, stared around the unit for his celly before hanging up the phone. Smooth was playing dominoes. Roman checked the time on his G-Shock watch, it read 8:37 pm. He had just enough time to release the heavy load his balls were carrying. Images and sounds of Diva fucking herself were still vividly flashing through his mind.

UP IN HIS CELL, Roman, put his privacy panel over his cell door window, grabbed his lotion, and laid on his bed. He preferred to use lotion rather than Vaseline because it made more of a wet-pussy sound. Pulling his pants right below his buttocks, he squirted lotion into his hand, grabbed a hand full of his prick, and began to jerk it. "Uh...Uh ... Uh," he moaned as he looked at
a picture of Diva bending over in booty shorts on his wall. "Let me fuck dat ass ... Let me fuck dat ass," Roman sexually chanted. He imagined Diva laying on her back naked, and him turning her over unto her stomach. Him pulling her up from her waist, and fucking her from the back. "Slssh-slssh-slssh-slssh," Sounded his hand sliding up and down his steel-like pole.

"Ugh, yes! Yes! Yes!"
Then he imagined sticking his tongue between Diva's fleshy bum, lubing it with saliva, and then rubbing the crown of his penis from her wet pussy to her tight asshole a few times, "Ah shit. I'm fuckin' dat ass ... Ah shit," Roman moaned, remembering how he used to fuck Diva in her ass. Lacing his fingers in between her's as she gripped the bed sheets, begging for more and more. Hearing Diva moaning in his imagination, Roman could feel a sensation vibrating up through his scrotum, up through his shaft, and his eyes

began to short circuit and roll to the back of his head. "Slssh-slssh-slssh-slssh," the rhythm of his jerk sped up until white glaze-like cum shot out of his dick on to his six-pack. His ass clinched several times as more and more of the creamy substance oozed out of his dick on to his hand. Inhaling deeply, Roman, shook his head, and looked down at the mess he made. "Damn, I love you, wifey," he said as he looked over at Diva's pictures looking back at him. "I love you too, hubby," he could hear her saying in his head.

CHAPTER 10 NIGGA ON THE RUN

Rafaella "Ella" Pearson called her two children to eat at the dining room table of her New Stanton Heights home. Through hard work, and lots of overtime at her Daycare job, she saved up every pen she could, participated in a Home Owner's Program, got a loan, and purchased her new house.

Earlier that day, she took her kids swimming, and now she was at home cooking. She was beat, and couldn't wait to relax and have a glass of wine.

Sitting box juice on the tabled, she watched her kids begin to eat. Then she gathered the dirty dishes, put them in the sink. After pouring dish liquid over them, she turned the hot water on and let it run over the pots and pans in the sink.

KNOCK-KNOCK-KNOCK-KNOCK!

The sound of knocking at her front door startled her, and made her jump. She had just moved, and she had only given a few people her new address so the beat of the knock at her front door surprised her.

Wiping her hands on her pants, she asked, "Who is it?!"

"It's me, open the door!"

"Me who?!" Ella asked, walking to the door at a slow pace.

"GRINCH!" Grinch said, looking around into the dark that surrounded the home. His head was on swivel from the paranoia of killers tracking him.

Hearing Grinch say his name made Ella pick her pace up, and answer the door, "What are..." Started saying as Grinch busted through the door past her.

"What are you doin' here?! I told you to call first," Ella said, standing with the door open. "Plus, I don't want you over here this time of night. Ya kids are about to go to bed," She continued.

"Daaaddy..."

.Daaaddy...Daddy!" Coming out of the kitchen to see who their mother was talking to they were pleasantly surprised to see their father, unlike their mother.

"Shut the door, Ella. Shut the door, and lock that ma'fucka," Grinch said in between deep breaths. His kids Held him at the waist, looking up to him.

"But...

"...SHUT DA FUCKIN' DOOR!" Grinch demanded, making Ella shut her door.

"What's goin' on. Why are you breathing all hard?" Ella asked, sensing something was wrong. "You two go finish eatin!" She told their kids.

"Put dem to bed, and we'll talk. Some shit went down and dis is the only save place I could come to," Grinch told Ella, wiping beads of sweat from his forehead.

"Save place?! What did you do?!" Ella asked. If she would have checked her messages she would have known that her baby daddy had beat Evette half to death, and his best friend had been shot and killed. But her cellphone was dead inside her travel bag upstairs in her house, somewhere.

"Like I said we'll talk, once the kids are in bed. Here, take dis," Grinch said, lifting his long white tee, taking a five-gee stack from his bulging pockets, and extending it to her.

"Where'd you get that. I don't want that!" Ella backed up from Grinch, saying.

"Quit being stupid. Take dis money, man." Grinch said, stepping up on Ella.

"Mommy, we're finished. Can we play with daddy?" Grinch's daughter, Misty, asked. She was standing alongside her little brother, Clayton.

"Not tonight, princess. We'll play tomorrow. Okay?" Grinch told his daughter, picking her up. She wrapped her arms around her father's neck, and rested her head on his shoulder.

ON THE WESTSIDE OF PITTSBURGH,

Blonde and Dice pulled up to the transport spot, each one of them carrying a Hefty Bag full of Exotic ITSVIM. Evette was laying on the couch when they walked in, "What happened," she asked as she sat up. "What da fuck is dat?!" Washer next question when she saw the bags in their hands.

"We didn't see him," Blonde spoke up, and said, dropping he bag to the floor.

"Dis ah I'll gift fo' you," Dice said, dropping his bag to the floor as well. Evette was all over it, "Bitch, I knew you would handle ya business," Evette said, with a smile on her face, and pulling a couple pounds from the thick, black bag. With her head cocked to the side, she extended her arms, and hugged Blonde, "Thank you, sis'!"

"Fo' real, we didn't see him," Blonde said, making Evette stand back, and study the expression on her face for lies. Something was different about her, First, Dice noticed it, and now Evette did, too.

"You good?!" Evette asked. Dice just stood back, and watched the two of them. He was surprised that Blonde didn't trust Evette with the news of her killing Ew-Wee for the sake of her.

"Nn...Nnnn ... Yo?!" Roman, answered his cellphone. Breaking up the awkwardness that was overcoming the room.

"I'm out front, pullin' up," Diva told Dice.

"Cool. The door is open," Dice said to Diva. "Give me dat jawn," Dice said to Blonde, asking for the murder weapon. Blonde lifted her hoodie, and handed the chrome forty-five to him. "Seriously, you a'ight, yo?!" Dice asked again, he was feeling the way she was acting.

"Why y'all keep askin' me dat shit?! I told y'all I'm straight. I just need ah blunt, an' shit. Roll some'in' up, bitch!"

Blonde turned and said to Evette,

"Got some'in' already rolled.!"

"WASSSSUP, BITCHES?!" Diva came in the spot saying, holding up two bottles of Cîroc.

"Sasses!" Seeing Diva made Blonde lighten up. Dice had introduced the two of them shortly after he met her.

"Oooh shiiit! Baby, daaamn, What in da fuck! Oh, dat nigga gots tah die!" Diva stomped around, wit her head panning side to side, and a grit om her face. "Bro ... Yo, bro, why dis nigga ain't dead, yet?!" Seeing Evette face made her go berserk.

"Oh, we gon' get him, believe dat!" Dice said as he •lit the blunt Evette handed him.

Our Love Is A Life Sentence

"Da streets are watching, so we gotta be careful, but dat nigga gotta go!" Diva said, putting her knuckles to her teeth. "Let me look at you, baby," she continued, walking up to Evette, and examining her face. "Mm mm mm," she hummed, closing her eyes, and walking away from damage Grinch had caused.

"Here, sis," Blonde handed Diva the blunt.

"What da fuck is dis?!" Diva asked, looking in to one of the garbage bags sitting on the floor. "Oh, we 'bout to get high as ah ma'fucka!"

"Hmph!" Dice grunted, with a devilish grin stretched across his face.

"Y'all got wraps, don't y'all?" Diva asked.

"Plenty of 'em. We got like ah case of dem bitches," Blonde said.

"Well, let's roll up, and pour out. Ma'fuckas den took my king away from me, too. Bitches, I'm ready to get fucked up! Hey tho, it's crazy about dat nigga Ew-Wee gettin' smoked, ain't it?" Diva said, in between pulls of the blunt.

"Ew-Wee got smoked?!" The news was new to Evette,

"Hell yea, girl. Hol' up, y'all jacked dat nigga La' dig shit, didn't y'all," Diva was trying to put shit together. Dice never copped as much weed as she was looking at. It was two bags full of pounds.

"Nah sis', we ain't jack dat nigga. We went ova dat niggas spot to cop, and to see if he knew where Grinch was, and da door was cracked open. I think some niggas dig ah door-kick or some'in'. But yo, I look in, and I see some bags left behind, an' shit. Whoever jacked dat nigga must have got sooo much shit they had to leave dis shit behind. Anyway, we grabbed dat shit, and we got the fuck gone," Dice laid out an elaborate lie to avoid him exposing what really went down with a full clip. She had pulled the action of her firearm moved by the finger, releasing the firing pin until the slide kicked back. It had been many years from her first kill, but when given the reason to take an adversaries last breath, she did it without hesitation. Dom P. told her if she ever had to murk ah nigga to never leave a witness. "It's betta they die then they testify!"

He nagged through an internal voice in the back of Blonde's head.

Dominant "Peanut" Chambers was never supposed to die. He was just supposed to be robbed. Blonde had got mad at him because she had sold most of his work for him, and he refused to pay her. He told her that he was putting all the money back in to the flip, but Blonde didn't understand that. She was new to the game. But it was the same concept she used to come up with later in her life. But back then she felt like he was trying to play her. So, she set him up to get robbed. But in the process of him getting jacked, Dom P., refused to give up his money, so the jacker, shot and killed him.

Blonde's thought transference unveiled emotional scars that had never healed. So, tried her best to keep them all bottled up inside. Her mind raced at a high-speed pace, flashing scenes of both shootings.

Her gaze in to the abyss, and articulate and perceptive thoughts caused a ripple across her face, her nostrils flared, and her head and her head heated up. Pressure and tension, the feeling of being trapped had been responsible for her mental anguish and displeasures.

At that moment, it was like she had changed her life's views through every reverence. All in a matter of minutes. The thought of her putting in work for the team, and Dice just jetting off and leaving her to go home to his fat ass girl made her furious.

"Fuck 'em, Fuck 'em all. They'll all get what they deserve," she spoke through clinched teeth about every man in her life, gripping tight to the Smith & Wesson 9mm with the two-tone Polymer frame and stainless-steel barrel and slide.

WHILE BLONDE WAS AT HOME, tripping in the darkness of her bedroom, Dice, was working angles. Trying to make sure that he had covered all bases, and that Ew-Wee's murder wouldn't trail back to them. He also created a new lead that would cause Grinch to panic and get killed, or get captured and locked in to a cell for the rest of his natural life. Either way, Dice would be rid of him.

Our Love Is A Life Sentence

ROMAN'S MOTHER'S HOUSE, was located at a project complex in McKees Rocks, called the Manor. It was also on the Westside. It was an area of multi-leveled apartment buildings, littered with drug activity, pushers and murderers of all sorts. Luckily, Dice, was well known and respected there. As he pulled up in front of apartment building 3D, he caught the attention of a group of hustlers posted on the block, "Dice, what up, bro?!" One hustler called out.

"What's good, you a'ight," Dice asked.

"I'm a'ight, but I'd be betta if I had ya hand."

"Ha ha ha," the hustler said, then he and his homies chuckled.

"Shit, I'll give you ah hand anytime you need it, fam'. Matter of fact, I'ma stop through tomorrow, and make sure y'all boys are a'ight," Dice stopped, and told the corner boys.

"Aw man, that'll be what's up," the hustler responded. "Aye yo, you hear about Ew-Wee?" He asked Dice as he began to walk again.

"Yea. Man, dat shit's crrraaa-zy. I heard his own man did dat shit," Dice stopped in his tracks.

"Who?!" The hustler asked.

Our Love Is A Life Sentence

"Dat nigga Griz-zinch," Dice purposely put Grinch's name in the mix. Knowing what the young hustlers would do with the information, but he was just starting with putting Grinch's name in the air.

"Naaaah?!" The hustler was surprised by the accusation, but he half-ass believed what he was hearing.

"I don't know. I just heard dat," Dice said as he climbed several

steps, and disappeared in to the brick apartment building.

"You think dat nigga Grinch would do some'in' like dat," the

hustler asked his homies.

"You never know," one said.

"Fuck all dat. You think dat nigga gon' come through tomorrow?" Another hustler said.

"If he don't we just gon' jack dat nigga next time he comes through the hood," the hustler said, looking at the black SUV lit a glow from the street light beaming down on it.

KNOC-KNOCK ... KNOCK-KNOCK.

Dice knocked on Roman's Mother's door.

"Hey brother..."

"Who's that?!" Syria answered the door, and her mother asked who was there.

"It's me, ma. Dice." Dice answered.

"Heyyy Dice," Roman's mother, Marielle said, coming from the kitchen to hug and kiss him. "You okay, on?" She asked.

"Yea, ma. You?"

"Just tired. I talked to you brother, Roman, earlier," She told Dice. "Yea, how is he? I was just wit' Diva."

"He's gon' be okay, he's strong,' Marielle reminded Dice as well as herself.

"Yea, he is, ma."

"Okay, I'm goin' to bed. That lil boy ran me crazy today," she said about lil Roman.

"Ha ha, yea?"

"Yes lawd," Marielle said, walking in to her bedroom where little Roman laid sleep in his dinosaur PJs.

"What's up, Dice?! I'm try'na get dat stack. What I gotta do?" Syria asked, in a whisper.

"Just make a few phone calls."

"Awl dat's easy money. Who you want me to call?"

"First, I need you to call the police."

"What?! The po-po?! Nah!"

"I need you. Sis, need you, too..." Dice paused, and looked Syria in the eyes, "Nobody's gon know. Ya not gon' leave ya name or nothin'. Just make an anonymous call. But you can't tell anybody you doin' dis. You can't even tell Diva."

"And I get ah stack?"

"Yea," Dice pulled out a stack, and handed it to Syria, it but you can't tell Nooo-body. Dat's part of the deal."

"Oh, you know I know how to keep ah secret," Syria said, stretching her bubble gum from her mouth, and twirling it around as she gave Dice the googly eyes. Hinting about the times they fucked, and she never said a word to anyone about it. That was also a part of another arrangement they had. Long as she kept her mouth shut, Dice, would buy her something or give her a couple dollars after they fucked.

"Aight, what I gotta say?"

"Look, I have to drive somewhere first. When I get there I'ma call you then you call and report the murder..."

"...A MURDA? What the hell are you gettin' me in to, Dice?!"

"You're not gettin' in to anything because no one is gonna know it was you dat call unless you tell them. Syria, ya gon' be good. Here, take dis," Dice pulled out a flip burn out cellphone, and gave it to Syria.

"Don't make the call here. The police will trace it here. Go to the Northside n' make the call," Dice told Syria, making sure that it was clear to her that if she slipped up she would lead the police straight to her.

"Might. So, you want me to go now?" Syria asked, stuffing the thousand dollars in to her pocket.

"Nah, wait. 'til I call you. Then go over. After you make the call, take the chip out of the phone, and destroy it. Do not keep the phone. After you make the 9-1-1 call they'll be able to trace it to wherever you go. Oh, before you go make a couple calls to some of you girls, the ones that can't keep a secret. Tell 'em that you heard that Grinch killed Ew-Wee."

"Huh? Grinch killed Ew-Wee?!"

"Dat's what I heard."

'Wight. What exactly am I tellin' the cops?" Syria asked.

"Call and tell 'em that you want to report a murda. Tell 'em Grinch robbed and shot him Then hang up, and take the battery out of the phone. They can't trace it with the battery out of it."

"Might, got it. Let me make a few calls. Once you hit me I'll go to the Northside, and make the call." Syria said.

The plan was set. It was a bitch move as some would say. Back in the days, Dice, would have never thought of doing anything like this, but this was a new era, and the game was being played differently. Hustlers were playing cutthroat, taking out and eliminating each other by any means. It was a deadly game, and he was playing for keeps.

After leaving Marielle's, Dice, drove to the Bottoms, another project section in Mckees Rocks. It was a couple minutes from the Manor.

Parking his SUV, Dice, took the murder weapon out of his stash, walked to a dock that sat on the river bank and threw it in to the murky waters.

Back in his SUV, he pulled up the iPhone Locator app, and checked Grinch's whereabouts. He was still at the same location. Dice hit the parkway and headed eastbound.

Twenty minutes later, Dice, drove in to Stanton Heights. The red dot on the phone locator blinked steadily as he drove through the gracious residential streets and comfortable, well-to-do homes.

BLINK-BLINK-BLINK

The red light progressed, and began to blink more rapidly. Finally, Dice, had located the exact home Grinch was located at.

"Should I just lay on dis nigga, or should I call the phone, wait fo' him to come out of the house, and kill him? Naaah!" Dice said to himself before he made the call to Syria.

It seemed to be his best plan at the time. Besides that, he couldn't risk being in a shootout in the area. The cops would be all over him. Picking up his cellphone from his lap, he called Syria, "Go 'head, make the call, and tell 'em you think he's at the address. I'm about to text you," Dice told Syria, texting Ella's house number to her.

"Nnn ... Nnn ... Nnn," Blonde's phone lit up in the dark. Laying there in her bedroom alone, her fully operating mind seemed incapable of sleep. Looking at the LCD screen, she didn't recognize the number so she let the caller go to voicemail until her cellphone vibrated again, "Who's dis?!"

"It's me, Dice. Open the door," Dice had got rid of his burner phone, and activated another. He was crossing all his tee's and dotting his I's.

"Snst ... Snst," Blonde opened the door with tears in her eyes. "Yo, what's up?! You cool," Dice wrapped his arms around Blonde.

"Snst ... 1 didn't think you were coming over," Blonde said, sniffling.

"Nah bae, .1 just had to go tie up some loose ends. We good now. Now we can chill, and get back to the money," Dice told Blonde

as held her. But chilling would be the last thing on their agenda. In the Manor, word had got back to another notorious Westside baller about who had killed his cousin, Ew-Wee, and who had said it.

CHAPTER 11 SNAKES

THE NEXT MORNING AFTER BREAKFAST, yard was called, but Roman stayed in. He wanted to meet with his counselor to see what jail he was designated to. Smooth went to the yard to meet with Banks. It was the only place besides the chow that they could meet up.

"You hear anything else from your lawyer, bro?" Smooth asked Banks as they walked the yard.

"Not yet. Man, I'm try'na get outta dis bitch, fo' real!" Banks said to his homie. You hear anything?"

"Feel you. My moms said my lawyer's supposed to call dis mornin'. So I'ma hit her around lunch time, an' see what he talkin' 'bout. Shit, I'm tired of doin' time already."

"Ha ha ha," Banks chuckled. "When we get out what da fuck we gon' do?" He asked.

"What you mean?"

"You know, house arrest an' shit. How we gon' get back to dat paper," Banks inquired, looking at his friend with steel eyes. "I'm workin' on some'in' now."

"Oh yea, what?!"

"Dis nigga Roman eatin', he gettin' dat paper in dis bitch, an' I know if he hustlin' in here then he got some paper out there somewhere.

"Prolly do."

"I know dis nigga do."

"So how is dat gon' help us?"

"If I get dis niggas address, or number I'ma kidnap dat nigga's bitch. I'ma get to dat paper."

"Hmph, sounds like ah plan. Ah good one, too. All we gotta do is get out.

"Shit, even if only one of us get out we gotta move on dis."

"Definitely."

"How you plan on gettin' close to his bitch?"

"It's gon' be hard. Far as what Roman tells me about the bitch, she's loyal, and ah straight rider.

"Oh, so you ain't gon' be able to fuck the bitch."

"I wish I could dat bitch bad as fuck!"

"Oh yea. Yo, let me ask you dis, how much bread you think dat nigga got.? Is dis shit gon' be worth it?!"

"Dat nigga try'na open ah rental car spot, and before he got locked up, he sold ah couple pieces of property. He was tellin' me the Fed's couldn't fuck wit' dat gwuap cause the property was in his bitches name. So, I know he sittin' on some'in' nice."

"Then all we gotta do is get at the bitch. Did you ask dat nigga 'bout any work?"

"Nah. I just been listening to dat nigga, lettin' him talk an' shit. Nigga been talkin' to me like I'm some young, dumb nigga." "Hell yea. Where he at? Why he ain't come out?"

"He in there try'na find out where he's goin'."

"Oh, he 'bout to leave?"

"Yea, he might leave next week. He might go before I go to court."

"I go tomorrow. Hopefully these ma'fuckas free me."

"They gon' let you go, fam'. Man, I had forgot dat quick dat you were goin' down tomorrow."

"Well, like I said, tho, if you get out an' I don't, I'ma send you dudes info, an'. we work from there."

"Bet! What's his bitch's name. I'ma see if my bitch knows her. "Diva, she from the Westside."

AN HOUR HAD PASSED, and inmates made their way back inside of the prison to their Units from the yard. "A'ight bro, I'll see you at lunch," Smooth said to Banks as they parted ways. Smooth was going to wait to call his mother, but curiosity got the best of him.

"Hello?" His mother answered.

"Hey ma, did the lawyer call?" Smooth asked.

"Yes. He said that it would be in your best interest to cooperate." "What?!" Smooth looked around at the other inmates on the phone, there were only a couple.

"What he say about gettin' me out on bail?"

"He said that's not going to happen unless you cooperate."

"Dat's crazy," Smooth paused and said as the guy next to him on the phone hung up. The other guy was on the opposite side of him. He looked around to make sure nobody listened, and then whispered, "So if I snitch they'll let me out?"

"Yup. He said there's this thing called Queen For A Day..."

"Queen For A Day, what the hell is that?"

"They'll call you down to questioned you, and if they like the information you give them they'll cut your time, and get you out on bail."

I'M," Smooth paused for several seconds, "And if I don't do dis I gotta stay here?" Smooth asked, looking around.

"At least until you go to court, and he said that could be two years or more."

"I know," Smooth thought about how long Roman said it took him to go to court. "So when are they try'na do this?"

"They'll do it the day you go for you bond hearing so no one suspects anything, and after you sit down with them they'll have

your bond hearing. If they like the information you give them they'll have a mock-trial type of thing..."

"A mock-tail, what's dat?'

"...It's when they act like they're having a hearing, but your fate is already determined. It's just something to make things look good." "These ma'fuckas are vicious!"

"So, what you want me to tell them," Smooth's mother asked. "What you think, ma?"

"I want you to come home," Smooth's mother said.

"Might, tell 'em I'll do it, but only if I get bail."

"He said if you do it you'll get bail because they want you to get some more information out here."

"A'ight. Love you."

"Love you, too. I'ma call the lawyer back now. He's waiting on your answer.

"Okay ... CLICK!" Smooth check to see if anyone had overheard his conversation, but everyone was preoccupied with doing time.

Smooth walked away from the phones, slowly. He felt like shit. He never thought that he would be in a position that would make him become a Federal Informant, but he was doing it for his mother. At least that's what he told himself. He wondered if Banks was offered the same deal. If he was he would definitely be out the next day. "Should I do this shit ... Fuck it. I'm try'na get outta this bitch," he thought, climbing the steps to the second tier.

Our Love Is A Life Sentence

IN HIS CELL, Roman laid on his bunk reading the USA Today newspaper. "Wassup bro, they tell you where ya going?" Smooth asked Roman.

"USP Canaan," Roman said, putting his newspaper to the side, and sitting up.

"What they say dat join's like," Smooth went on.

"My man said it's a lot of New York dudes up there. Beside.dat he didn't really know.

"When you think you gon' be leavin'," Smooth probed.

"The cousnselor said it will be next week or the week after, fo' sho. The nigga out pretty quick. They try'na make room."

"Damn. I gotta give you my info before you go."

"Yea, I'll give you mines too. I hope they let you out dis bitch, so you can get'cha money up fo' ah lawyer."

"Yea, I'ma definitely need to do dat," Smooth said. "And kidnappin' ya bitch is gon' help me get straight, nigga," he thought to himself.

"I might have a homie dat might look out fo' you, help you get back on ya feet."

"Oh yea, dat's what's up."

"I don't know, I'll see. He might be out there chillin', I'll let you know, tho."

"Bet

"Hey, let's go ova some of the shit you need to know about ya bond hearing.

'Wight," Smooth said, sitting down at a small steel table in the cell. "I ain't gon' needed, tho. I'm already gettin' out," Smooth thought.

"Like I said, they gon' try to deny you because of your pendin' case, but you have ya lawyer use dat to ya advantage. Tell him to tell 'em dat you've already been out on parole reporting and goin' to every court date. Also, they're goin' to try to say dat you're

a threat to the community, but tell ya lawyer to fight dat by sayin' dat you have only one pendin' case dat you haven't been convicted of yet."

The more Roman spoke about the bond hearing the more he helped Smooth make up his mind, he was definitely going to be queen of the day or whatever else the Feds wanted him to be. He had a plan to get some money, and him being locked up wasn't going to stop him from getting it.

As Roman was putting Smooth down with how to have his lawyer address the court, Diva, was picking up little Roman from his grandmother's. Before she left, her and the twenty-two year old she called her sister, "Syria," sat on the apartment building stoop, and smoked a blunt.

"Shit's crazy 'bout Ew-Wee, ain't it?" Diva said, inhaling the weed, and looking over the blunt as she exhaled.

"Yea Dice..." Syria started to tell Diva about the move she made for Dice, but stopped.

"Dice, what?"

"Nothin'..."

"Nah bitch, what?!"

"Dice said dat Grinch did it," She switched up what she was about to say.

"Yeah, I heard. Crazy!"

"Sis, I miss my brutha so much," Syria said. But at least I know he's safe where he's at," Syria said, not understanding that people in jail could be killed just as easy as those in the streets. Your chances of survival depended on what jail you were in, and your background.

"I miss my hubby, too. Once he moves I'll take you to see him," Diva told Syria.

"Yes, I really need to see my bro."

"I got you," Diva said, passing the blunt.

As Diva and Syria talked, Head Homicide Detective, Francis Tompkins, read a sticky note left on his desk the night before.

It was pertaining to the information Syria gave a 9-1-1 dispatcher.

"Al, we gotta lead on that homicide on the Westside last night. Let's go check it out," he told his partner, Albert Gnocchi, handing him the sticky note.

"Grinch? That's the name those females gave us last night. He's one of the guys they were going to hook up with," Detective Gnocchi said, reading the name in parentheses on the small lime sticky sheet.

"Let me pull his name up, see who we're dealing with.

TAP-TAP-TAP-TAP-TAP-TAP

Detective Tompkins fingers stabbed the computer keyboard, and within seconds he got two hits.

"This would be our guy, "Lucas Sanford, being that the given address is on the Westside," the detective assumed. If the detectives would have done. their homework the night before they would have known this information already.

"The address on the sticky note is in Stanton Heights, should we get a body warrant?" Detective Gnocchi asked.

"Nah, let's just go over there and ask for the guy. See what kind of response we get," Detective Tompkins said, pressing print on the computer screen to print out a colored mugshot of Grinch.

"This note is saying that this guy killed our victim; the females are saying that they were all going out on a date; my question is why would a man kill his friend right before they were supposed to go on a hook up," Detective Gnocchi questioned.

"And if he was already in the house, once he killed his friend, why didn't he take the three-hundred thousand dollars we found. He had to know about the illegal activity that was going on there. Within the first several minutes of being inside of the house we found ounces of weed, and it smells like some high-grade weed," Detective Tompkins added.

"You would know, wouldn't you," he snorted.

With a devious laugh Tompkins responded, "I'm just saying partner. Something's not adding up here."

"Well, maybe we'll get some answers once we question this guy. One thing for certain, though," the detective paused, "he didn't stick around, or call the murder in."

"If you were on federal probation would you," Detective Tompkins asked, looking over at his partner.

THE NIGHT BEFORE, Danielle Wilkins and Missy Brown, drove across the West End Bridge from the North Side to an apartment on the West End, "Girl, this call came right on time. I needed to smoke," Missy said.

"Who you tellin, and if we lucky we'll be able to get ah couple dollars off these niggas."

Giggling just a little too loud she exclaimed, "Oh, I'ma fuck my nigga to sleep, an' get all up in dem pockets."

"You be doin' dat shit too?" Danielle asked in amusement. She smiled as she could relate.

"Fuckin' right I do! Slow ma'fuckas don't even be knowing."

"What's the most you hit ah nigga fo'?" Danielle asked as she rubbed her hands together, she could almost feel the cash in her hands.

"I don't know, like five hunid."

Missy stopped to think for a minute, putting her fingers to her temple before blurting out, "FIVE HUNID?!" She waited to see Danielle's reaction before responding again. "Yea girl. Plus, I got high, got fucked really good, and he broke me off like three hunid."

Dat's the nigga we 'bout to go see, he is eatin', girl."

"You think we gon' be able to hit 'em up tonight?" Danielle asked.

"Well, I know Ew-Wee got dat bag. I don't really know the one you hookin' up wit'. I heard of Grinch and seen him ova there a few times, but I don't know what his pockets is sittin' like."

"What he look like? Do he look like he balm'? Is he cute?"

"Bitch, what do you care about him bein' cute? We try'na get high, and if we could, get ah couple dollars outta these lames."

"You right!"

"When I seen him, he was coppin' some bud off Ew-Wee, so he might be gettin money. At least he's gettin' enough to pinch from," she fell out in laughter again.

"O-Kaaaay?!" Danielle high fived her friend and laughed with her. They were ready for whatever.

Danielle and Missy believed that they were going over Ew-Wee's house to have a good time, but when they got there the door was ajar.

A trail of blood was leading to the body of one, "Donald "Ew-Wee" Portland Seeing Ew-Wee's nearly decapitated body sent the two gold-diggers into a frenzy. Their screams screeched and cut through the night's quiet. Gaining her composure, Missy, called the police and was told not to leave the scene. After being questioned by detective's Gnocchi and Tompkins, they were finally let go. There was not much information they could provide. Besides their motives for meeting with the two, they were to hook up with investigative reports.

FOLLOWING THEIR LEAD, detectives Gnocchi and Tompkins knocked on the door of a house in Stanton Heights, "BOOM-BOOM-BOOM-BOOM," Detective Gnocchi banged on the door.

"WHO IS IT'?" Ella asked, with an irritated voice

"Detective's Tompkins and..." Ella unlocked her front door and swung it open as the detective was announcing their names, " Detective Gnocchi. How are you?" the detective asked Ella.

"I would be better if you weren't bangin' on my damn door!" Ella said.

"Can we come in," Detective Tompkins asked Ella.

"NO!"

"Do you know him," detective Tompkins asked, showing the colored mugshot of Grinch.

"Yeah, I know that no good ma'fucka. He ain't shit. That's my baby-daddy'"

"Have you seen him?" Detective Gnocchi asked.

"No! I wanna see him. He was supposed to bring my kids some shoe and outfit money yesterday, and he stopped answerin' his phone. Why what's goin' on? Why y'all showin' his jail picture? Did he violate his parole again?"

"Not yet. Can we have his number?" Detective Tompkins asked.

"I don't feel comfortable giving the po-po my baby daddy's number. We 'already havin' issues."

"You say you have a baby by him," Detective Tompkins asked, trying to look beyond Ella into her home. As he did so, Ella, pulled her door shut, and, stepped out on the porch.

"We'll we're investigating an homicide, and we have information that states that Lucas was the last to see our victim," Detective Tompkins said.

"Homicide ... Victim, who got killed?" Ella asked.

"You haven't been watching the news young lady," Detective Tompkins asked, staring at her with a hard expression.

"No! 'I hate the news'. Eh' time I watch it someone I know is dead." Unfortunately, it was the same this time. She knew Ew-Wee well, he was there at the hospital when her last child was born, and always attended her cook outs. Hearing Ella's explanation of why she didn't watch the news, and Ella thinking about her friend's death, made them all, grow quiet for a moment.

"Well, if Lucas shows up give him our card, or you call us. As of right now, he's just wanted for questioning, but if he doesn't •contact us soon we will have to put out a warrant for his arrest. You do understand, don't you? I don't want to take your kid's father away from them," Detective Tompkins said, knowing how hard it was on a young black single mother.

"Yeah, I understand. When he contacts me, I'll give him the message," Ella said, looking over the card.

"Okay, thank you," Detective Gnocchi said as the two detectives turn, and walked to their car.

"Gotdamn baby momma's fuckin' crazy," Detective Gnocchi said! Hmph, sadly, she doesn't have a clue," Detective Tompkins added, but little did the detectives know, Ella, had all the sense in the world. She was far from the dumb hood chick she had appeared to be to them.

Inside of her house, Ella, marched into her bedroom, "Mm mm, you gots to go, ma'fucka! You got homicide detectives coming to my fuckin house lookin' for ya ass!"

"Calm down," Grinch said, holding his kids in both arms on the bed. "Y'all go play while me and mommy talk," he. told them.

"YOU GOTTA GO!" Ella demanded with her hands on her hips as her two kids flew pass her.

"Ella, I can't leave right now. They might still be out there waitin' fo' me to leave, and you just lied to them. We'll both be in trouble!" Grinch stood up and tried to reason with Ella. "I'ma leave soon enough, just not right now."

"Man'" Ella's nostrils flared, and she shook her head, "You always caught up in some shit, Lucas!"

"Baby, I didn't do anything this time. ma' fuckas tried to kill me too I was almost gone

"Why don't you just turn yourself in, and tell them what happened?" "Because if I do I'm goin! back to jail on ah violation, and once

they get the forensics back on the gun I left behind I'ma have ah new case," Grinch said, leaving out the attempted homicide charge he would also be facing if Evette pressed charges.

"OH MY GOD, LUCAS!! You always fuckin' up!"

"Come here, man. I...," He paused, wrapping his arms around Ella's waist. She tried to pull away, but his grip was too strong around her. "...I know I be fuckin' up, but this time trouble found me. Whatever happens I'ma make sure you an' the kids are good, this time."

"You betta, because shit is hard as fuck out her with two kids," Ella said, looking Grinch in his eyes.

"Mmrnuu-ah, I got y'all,' Grinch kissed Ella and said. "Yo! But how the fuck they get'cha new address, ho?!"

"What you mean, they the police!"

Our Love Is A Life Sentence

"Nah Ella, they wouldn't be able to link me to ya new address. Ya old one, yeah, because the Fed's got it on file, but not this address. Some'in's ... Some 'in's crazy," Grinch said, letting Ella go, and walking away from her. Then Evette's iPhone caught his eye, "Yo! You think ah ma'fucka traced this phone to us?" Grinch asked.

"Let me see. Whose phone, is it?" Ella asked, examining the cell phone.

"Ew-Wee gave it to me," Grinch lied

"Maybe. It's ah iPhone, and iPhone got an app that you could use to trace the phone if it's stolen."

"Yeeaah"

"Yea!"

"I know this ma'fucka, dice ain't track me here, and have the police come at me," Grinch said under his breath, "Naaah!"

"What you say?" Ella asked as Grinch walked the iPhone into the bathroom, and ran it under water to short circuit it.

"What you doin'?!" Ella asked following behind Grinch.

"El', dem ma'fuckas tracked me wit' dis phone."

"Who? It couldn't have been the police because they would have came with a warrant, and busted in her instead of knockin'," Ella knew about the law a little bit She had learned by listening to Grinch talking about his old case, and by watching Law and Order.

"I don't know, El'," Grinch didn't want to tell Ella what he was thinking, but he knew Dice was behind the cops showing up there, somehow, some way. But why didn't dat nigga make a move on me Why the fuck did he send the cops" Grinch questioned "It had to be dat bitch, it couldn't have been Dice, nah" Grinch reasoned.

"Why are you talkin' to yourself," Ella questioned

"Look, I need you to go get me ah burn out I'ma be out tonight, and I need you to be able to get in touch with me. Just in case the police come again."

"They might be gettin' ah warrant now. They might be comin' back, baby!"

"Fuck! you right. look, go circle the block a couple times, and make sure dem ma'fuckas is gone So I can be out I'ma need ya whip

"What?!"

"I'ma need ya whip, man I'll drop it downtown at one of dem little parking spots, the one by George Aiken's You can pick it up there I'll get ah burnout, and call you."

"Alright, let me get my keys," Ella said.

"Hey babe, I think y'all should leave, too

"Boy, you crazy. Leave fo' what?!" Ella asked, but without Grinch telling Ella the full story she would not understand why Grinch felt that she and his kids could be in danger.

"Got 'em. I'll be right back, babe."

"A'ight. If anybody look suspicious be on point."

"Boy, I know what the police look like," Ella said, leaving out of the front door.

"I'm not just talkin' 'bout the police. Eh... Aw man, whhewww!

 Ma'fuckas bet not fuck wit' mines. I'll take him, his fat ass bitch, and they three lil niggas out," Grinch said, watching Ella pull off in her Buick Enclave through the windows of her front door.

AT BLONDE'S SOUTHSIDE SPOT, the sharp ring and vibration of Dice's new burner cell phone woke him Blonde laid beside him woke, with her eyes shut. *Cling-a-ling-a-ling. ....Nn nn....*

Sitting up, Dice, reached below the bed for his cell phone. It was in his Robin's Jeans. Pressing the side button, he illuminated the screen. Swiping his finger, he unlocked the screen. The missed call was from Evette, he had texted her his new number before he fell asleep. Pressing on the missed call of the number dialed, before it could ring twice, Evette Answered, "Big Bro, you ain't gon' believe dis shit," She said, anxious to tell of some news she had heard.
"What, 'Vette?!" Dice's muscles tensed, his back straightened, and Blonde's eyes opened as she turned over to look at Dice.
"5-0 found three-hunid stacks in dat boy Ew-Wee's spot."
"GET DA FUCK OUTTA HERE, 'VETTE" Dice's response really had Blonde's attention now.
"What, bae?" She asked, sitting up beside him.
"They found three-hunid racks in Ew-Wee's spot."
"Fuck outta here!" Blonde said.
"Dat right there is crazy," Dice said., looking at Blonde, sort of feeling like she dropped the ball, but so did Grinch as did Danielle and Missy. They had all watched the news

at. some point. Ella had told the homicide detectives that she did not watch the news, but that was a lie. Her and Grinch had watched the 5:30 am news after having sex that night. They were both awestruck finding out what Grinch had left behind. It had been a rough night, besides having sex with Ella, nothing good had came out of the night Ewwee's life was taken.

The money he had left behind was money he could have used to move himself and his family out of town, buy a new home, and start the business he always wanted to start up. Instead of checking the bedroom closet the three-hundred thousand was found in he had settled for a measly twenty thousand dollars. Now Dice was getting the news about the blunder. With the drugs and guns found along with the large sum of drug money no one would be able to claim the police 'bought out of the house on the news in the large Louie duffle bag.

"Dat would have been a nice come up," Dice said.

"Who you tellin'?! I'm about to hit the set, bro. When you comin' back through," Evette asked, wanting to know when Dice was going back to his spot.

"I gotta go to the crib. Then I'll be over. Why don't you wait 'til I get there before you leave? I need you to take care of some'in' fo' me."

"Where you at now?"

"Ova Blonde's ... What?!" Dice asked Blonde, reaching for her wrist as she got out of the bed, pulling away from him. He questioned her attitude, and couldn't figure out what upset her. Blonde was mad that he was going home to his woman.

"She trippin', huh?" Evette asked.

"Yea, but whatever, man.,' Dice said, shaking his head.

"She was acting weird as hell last night."

"Yea, she was, but she's cool."

"How long you gon' be bro. I'm try'na get back to this paper."

"Look 'Vette, you need to be careful. That nigga's still out there."

"Yea, and I'm try'na see him. I ain't runnin' from dat nigga I'm try'na run to him."

"Dat shit ain't work Out fo' you last time," Dice thought. "You just need to be careful out there. You haven't fully healed, yet. You just got outta the hospital yesterday."

"Like I said, how long you gon' be, bro?"

"'Bout an hour. I'ma go change clothes, and then I'll be ova," Dice said as Blonde turned on the water in the shower. Hearing the water running, Dice, figured that he would shower there, and Luck Blonde the way she wanted to be Lucked the night before, when he was too tired to have sex with her.

"Bro, just meet me at my house. I'ma go get change outta these bloody ass True's, and get my striz'nap."

"Check my dresser drawer, I got some'in' nice in there fo' you," Dice told Evette.

"A'ight. Meet you at my house," Evette said before hanging up with her. She didn't have time to be cooped up in some spot, and she definitely wasn't going to allow Grinch to run her off the block. She had money to make, and if any confrontation came her way she would be ready to handle it. Thinking about what Dice said, she went in to his bed room and checked where she knew he kept his protection. A gat was a necessary tool that was much needed in their line of work.

Wiping her hands on her pants before she opened the dresser drawer made her check her hands for blood. She had forgot about the blood that stained her pants, the hospital had cut her True Religion T-shirt off her, before taking her in to surgery. Standing at the dresser, she thought about running in to Grinch on the way home, and cringed.

A sense of fear surged through her body as she thought about the monster that had almost her, her life. Opening the

Our Love Is A Life Sentence

top dresser drawer, she lifted a neatly folded stack of white V-neck tee's, and there laid a Herstol and a Hi-Point 40sw .40 Caliber. She picked up the Hi-Point, and tucked it into her tight waistband, and set out to get money.

CHAPTER 12 MR. BIGGA FIGGA

Theartis "Bigga Figga" Scott was huge in stature, he stood 6'4", and weighed over three hundred pounds. His dark skin and cockeyes made people compare him to the late, great, Notorious B.T.G. His body was covered with jailhouse tattoos, his massive chest pecks bared two meaningful tat's, the right side was tatted with nine strikes, and his left was tatted with two separate dates; 9/24/08 and 4/11/2010. The nine strikes represented the killings he had under his belt, in-and-out of prison, and as the first cousin of Ewee he was looking foward.to adding the tenth or multiple strikes to the symbolic tat once he caught up to whoever killed his cousin. The dates represented the dates he was acquitted for murder, with the help of his Jewish lawyer's, and a few dozen shoulder length, dread-headed, pill-popping, lunatics. They helped him run the block that paved the way through The Manor. As a tight drug peddling-unit they terrorized other pushers on the strip that was a half of a block away from the Mckees, Rocks Police Station. Gathered around on the set, Rick Ross's Mastermind CD pounded from Bigga Figga's powder-blue, cream-color-gutted, Rolls Royce drophead coupe. Other cars like Camaro's and Challenger's, and a few bikes and Quad's were also parked there. Periodically, the police rode pass and gave the street goons a hard look, but never stopped. To them it wasn't worth the confrontation. With resident's scared to complain about the motorbike's and Quad's ripping up-and-down the Street as kids played, Bigga Figga and his crew were able to get away with disturbing the peace, and do whatever they wanted to do.

"Dat boy Dice is on his way down here," Timbo, a runner of Bigga Figga's said to him. He was one of the three hustlers that had hollered at Dice the night before. He worked for Bigga Figga, but Bigga Figga didn't sell bags so he allowed his crew to grab bags from other ballers. Long as they weren't copping weed or coc' from other ballers they weren't in violation. Something like that could cost them their lives, and with Bigga Figga's harsh street-rep', they knew not to cross him. Plus, Dice was a well established O.G. from the West, and had a reputation almost equal: to Bigga Figga's. The difference between the two was Dice didn't roll with a large entourage, and didn't brag about his kills by tatting them on his body. He knew that the police paid attention to those type of tattoos, and used them against a person at court.

"You said dat nigga said Grinch did dat shit, huh?" Bigga Figga asked Timbo.

"Hell yea. Dat's what dat nigga said," Timbo replied.

After Dice told the three hustlers that the night before, they went to Bigga Figga about it, but Bigga Figga had also heard about Grinch savagely beating Evette to a pulp, and wondered if Dice was just trying to put his cousin Ewee's death on Grinch.

"O.G. is smart like dat," Bigga Figga told himself. But regardless of whatever happened, Bigga Figga was going to get to the bottom of it. Fearless, and coldblooded, Bigga Figga was street and book-smart. He was the only hustler on the block that went to college. He had an academic and football scholarship. Succumbing to a knee injury during a tackle cost him a future NFL Draft.

Frustrated after a year of therapy, he dropped out of college, and became a full-fledge baller. With it came his first kill, then another and another. After beating two murder charges, he reigned as the king of his block. It was Ewee that had put him on. Their mother's were sisters, they had the same grandmother. When Blonde killed Ewee she didn't know this, and Dice did not think about it. Nor did he think about the possibility of going to war with Bigga

Figga, and he definitely didn't think about Grinch telling it all once he was apprehended. So there were a few things that he didn't consider, especially, Grinch going to Bigga Figga for refuge, and if he talked to the police, Dice and his she-thugs could get caught up in an investigation. Something that Roman was constantly advising him to stay away from.

After making a call to Timbo, and Timbo telling him that Bigga Figga wanted to holler at him, he began to think about all of these things, on his way home. As he thought about these things, he shook his head, and grabbed his cell phone off the leather console in his SUV to call his girl, Alex.

"Hey, stranger?! I missed you last night," Alex said, answering her cell phone.

"Hey, baby. Yea, I had some business to take care of."

"Eh'thang a'ight"

"Yea, eh'thang cool. Dice eased the slight-worry he heard in Alex's voice.

"It's sad what happened to Ewee," Alex said.

"Hell yea. Crazy!"

"He was so cool."

"Yea, he was. Did you pick up ya car, yet?" Dice switched the subject.

"No, I'm in the MKX. Me and the kids are on the way to the mall. Marlon needs new shoes so I'ma just get all three of them a couple pair, and some outfits for school.

"Fo' school?! School don't start till..."

"Dice, you know I don't wait till the last minute to do shit."

"I know, babe. You're a great wife and mother."

"Thank you, husband. Am I gonna see you tonight?"

"Yea. Prolly late, tho."

"Where you at now?"

"On my way home."

"Might. Love you."

"Love you, too. Oh, leave ya car at the parking garage for a couple more days. I'll let you know' when to go get it."

"Might. Just let me know." Alex said. After thinking about the things that he missed, Dice, needed to use his girls to do more dirt in. He had bought her the Malibu because it was a common car around the Pittsburgh area, and with him using the license-plate deflector it was easy for him to use it and get away with whatever crime he had committed.

Our Love Is A Life Sentence

AN HOUR LATER, OUTSIDE OF EVETTE'S HOUSE, "I'm out front. You ready?" Dice called Evette, and asked her.

"Yea. Give me ah few minutes," Evette told Dice, and a few minutes later she came out of the house.

"HUNK-HUNK!" Dice honked his horn to get Evette's attention, and hand motioned for her to come to him.

"What up, big bro," Evette asked, inside of Dice's SUV.

"Grab these."

"What's these fo'. I got work," Evette said, taking the three logs from Dice. A log was ten bricks of dope wrapped up in newspaper or Porno paper wrapped like these were.

"Dat's fo' dem fools down The Manor. I need you to follow me down there and be on point. Dat nigga Bigga Figga said he wanted to holla at me.

"'Bout what, dat Ewee shit?"

"Who knows, prolly so. Just watch my back."

"Dem ma'fuckas got dat shit set up like ah deathtrap, but I got you, you know dat!"

As Dice and Evette pulled up on the set, Timbo, twelve O'clock a four-wheeler down the block. Bigga Figga and his dread-headed hustlers watched from the small playground area on front street.

Our Love Is A Life Sentence

Dice pulled up, parked, and stepped out of his truck. Evette stayed in her car with the Hi-Point on her lap, checking her surroundings. She watched as Dice stood at the curb as Timbo whizzed a little pass him, and stopped at the drop of a dime, causing his two back wheels to pop up.

"What up, Dice?!"

"Yo, what up, bro?"

"You bring dat down fo' us?"

"You know I did. Go grab it off my girl. While I go holla at'cha man's," Dice said, motioning his thumb towards Evette.

'Wight, bet," Timbo said as him and Evette caught eyes.

"Give me $6750.00 back off dem joints, Dice told Timbo.

"Maaan, let us give you six-racks back, bruh!" Timbo said, offering

to give Dice an unreasonable amount back for his high-grade work.

"Nigga, give me sixty-seven-fifty. I be getting three-fifty ah piece of these joints. My work is fiyah. You know what it is!"

"Come look. Y'all want the shit or not?" Dice asked, looking at Timbo sideways.

"Look, let us give you sixty-two-fifty right now. No front. You know we gon' holla back," Timbo continued to negotiate. Dice looked at Timbo for several seconds. He knew he had to be firm with the youngin's. If he didn't they would think of him as being soft, but the play Timbo was offering was the right move to make. Though Dice didn't want to appear to be soft, he knew he had to compromise with the young wolves, or they would turn on him. 'Wight, let's do dat. Only fo' y'all, fam'."

"Good lookin', big bro. I got da bread on me right now."

"Cool. Holla at 'Vette," Dice said, extending his hand to Timbo. Timbo grabbed Timbo's hand and pulled him close. Walking over to talk to Bigga Figga, Dice, looked over his double-R drophead, "Stupid ma'fucka gotta Rolls Royce parked in the fuckin' 'jects. Makin' shit supa hot, an' shit," Dice mumbled to himself, walking up to Bigga Figga.

"What up, Dice? What it do, family, huh?!" Bigga Figga said, standing up out of his leather love chair he sat in on the block. When he got up he towered over Dice 5'9", muscular frame.

"What's the deal, my nigga Big-gash Fig-gah?!" Dice said as the two big homies shook hands, and embraced. Bigga Figga's hand swallowed Dice's. When Dice was pulled in to Bigga Figga he felt as though he was falling into a king-size mattress.

"Ha ha ha, you crazy Dice, man, huh?" Bigga Figga chuckled, watching Timbo approach Evette's ES 330, "Dat'cha girl dat Grinch pistol-whipped?" Bigga Figga asked Dice.

"Yeah yup, 'Vette," Dice replied, looking back at Evette as Timbo got into her car.

"Shit's crazy out here, but what can we do, tho, huh?"

"Make niggas pay fo' they sin's. Eye fo' an Eye's," Dice thought. "Yeah, I know, right," he said aloud.

"Daaamn, dat nigga Grinch did dat to you, slim?" Timbo asked Evette, caressing her hand. "I could handle dat fo' you, slim. Just say the word."

"Nah, I'm cool," Evette said, pulling her hand away from Timbo. Before he got in the car she tucked the .40 Caliber. She didn't want Timbo to feel threatened in any way, "Here you go, dis is three logs," Evette said reaching for a bag on her back seat.

Timbo looked Evette up-and-down as she reached for the bag on the back seat. He was really feeling her. Even with all the scars on her face.

"Here go da gwuap," he said, pulling the money he owed Dice out of his hoodie.

"What's up wit' you, tho? I'm try'na holla."

"You try'na holla?"

"Yeah. I'm try'na get wit' you. Take you to get something to eat or some'in'.

"We'll see, nigga. I wanna see what you do wit' dis work, first. Then you can holla. It's always business first wit' me, fam'."

"Oooh shit! I'm really try'na get wit' you. I'ma holla at you when I get down wit' dis work. That'll be like in ah hour, an' shit. So what's ya number," Timbo asked, pulling out his cell phone.

"You got Dice's number. Hit him when you down. I'm pretty sure he'll be sending me wit' mo' work. Dat is if you 'bout'cha business."

"Oh, I'm 'bout my business. I'm try'na be 'bout you too, tho."

"We'll see."

BACK TO DICE AND BIGGA FIGGA, "Hey, tho, Dice. My youngin's was tellin' me you heard Grinch killed my cousin," Bigga Figga said to Dice.

"I don't know if it's true, but I did hear that."

"From who?"

"Come on. fam'. You know 1 ain't..."

"From who, fam?" Bigga Figga said, in a much firmer voice.

"I know ya not in to name droppin', but this is about family." Bigga Figga said. If only he knew what Dice had done the night before. If he did know, Dice would have been shot dead right there on the spot.

"You right, fam'. Dat lil fiend bitch Betty told me, but she was prolly just runnin' her mouth, you know." Now Dice had to cover another lie. He would have to catch up with the fiend Betty before Bigga Figga's goons did. "I hope I ain't gettin' this bitch killed," Dice thought.

"Betty, huh? I'ma hav'tah holla at her. But how da fuck would she know dat, tho, huh?" Bigga Figga asked with a serious tone of voice. Making Dice feel uncomfortable.

"You know all fiends be knowin' all kinds of shit, but like I said, she might just be runnin' her mouth."

"Yeah, I guess they do, but it ain't like you to be spreadin' ah word of ah fiend."

"I was just sayin'. dat shit ain't the Commandment's, or nothin'. But you right, tho. I shouldn't said shit."

"Nah, I mean, you know, I'm just try'na find out who killed my people's. And before I start shootin' up shit I just wanna make sure I got my target's right, you know, huh?"

"Yeah, I feel you."

"Yeah. Hey bruh, you fuck wit' these?" After a few seconds of awkward silence, Bigga Figga said, pulling out a baggy of Xany-bars and Molly from his Polo jacket.

"Nah, I don't fuck around."

"What about dem hustlin' ass bitches you roll wit'?"

"Naaah, they cool, fam'," Dice said, shaking his head back and forth.

"What about dat Lean. I just got some from Philly. I'm 'bout 'tah turn the City out on dat shit. I could give you a deal on some pints," first Bigga Figga was trying to get Dice and his she-thugs high, and now he was try'na turn them on to the Syrup-game. The girls popped pills and took molly, but Dice wasn't going to expose their weakness to Bigga Figga.

'Wight. I'm just askin'. Hey tho, bruh, I'm fucked up 'bout cuz," Bigga Figga said thinking about his late cousin. "Y'all coming to the service?"

Our Love Is A Life Sentence

"I'm prolly not. I don't like dat type of shit. It fucks wit' me. The girls might come. I don't know."

"What about the wake?"

"I'll send flowers, Lam'."

"Hey, once I talk to Grinch I hope he don't say you an' ya bitches had anything to do wit' dis shit," the conversation between the two street gods began to take a turn.

"If he do, that ma'fuckas lyin'," Dice said, looking Bigga Figga in his eyes.

"Man, Ewee was ah good dude. He never did shit to me," Dice continued. Trying to convince Bigga Figga of his false innocence.

"Yeah. when's the last time you seen him?"

"The day before that shit happened. I grabbed like five pees off the homie."

"I never knew you was coppin' big like off my cuz. He never said shit to me 'bout it, huh."

"Nah, I just did that day fo' Roman's girl. He just got hit wit' ten, an' shit. He wanted to hit her wit' some'in' to help her keep the bills paid, you know?"

"I heard about dat nigga gettin' ten, and not sayin' shit to dem ma'fuckas. He ah stand-up nigga. But I thought you was handlin' business fo' him?"

"I am, but you know how broads are."

"Yeah. They be on dat bullshit."

"Yeah, hey. tho, I gotta go take care of some other shit.

"Oh yeah, my fault, fam'," Bigga Figga said, extending his hand. Dice grabbed it and shook it. Bigga Figga tightly gripped his hand, and wouldn't let it go, "How's ya girl Alex?"

"She's good," at this point the two street gods were no longer shaking hands but Bigga Figga still held Dice hand. "Hm ... Oh, my fault, damn," Bigga Figga expressed, finally, letting Dice's hand go. But Dice could still feel the pressure of Bigga Figga huge mitt holding his.

"I hope you find whoever did that to cuz. If I hear anything I'll hit you ASAP," Dice said before he walked off. Bigga Figga just nodded his head in silence and watched as Dice got in his truck, and pulled off with Evette behind him.

"What dat nigga say" Timbo walked up to Bigga Figga, and asked.

"Some bullshit, huh. Some'in' ain't right. I don't know what it is,

but some'in' ain't right. Anybody heard anything from dat nigga Grinch?" Bigga Figga asked.

"No, nab. Not yet."

"Don't change phones dis week. hold on to dat burner, just in case he tries to reach out, an' get at you."

'Wight, I just get another one, and hold on to dis one."

"Anybody got his girl's new address? I know she just moved outta the hood, an' shit."

"No, nope, but we gon' get it."

"Yeah, get it. Dat's prolly where dat nigga's at. Look, in ah minute ah nigga's gon' run outta patience. Ma'fuckas gonna turn me into "anybody killa. So you need to try harder to find dis nigga fo' the wrong ma'fuckas die," Bigga Figga said, taking some Molly, and chasing it with a bottle water.

Our Love Is A Life Sentence

BACK IN FRONT OF EVETTE'S HOUSE, "Here you go. Here's the paper dat nigga Timbo gave me," Evette said to Dice. "What was dat nigga Bigga talkin' 'bout?" She asked. "You know, 'bout Ewee. He try'na find out who killed him. He try'na find that nigga Grinch to get some answers. He can't get no answers from that nigga tho. You feel me?"
"Oh, if I come across dat You know what they say, dead niggas tell no tales. If I come across that nigga first he ain't gon' be sayin' shit."
"Hell yeah," Dice said as he sunk back into his seat, wondering how much time it would be before Grinch resurfaced.

CHAPTER 13 THE CROSSOVER

IN THE VISITING ROOM AT NEOCC, Roman watched Diva as she slowly walked up to the visiting booth. She wanted to give Roman time to look over her well-structured frame. Roman smiled and shook his head. As Diva sat down they picked up the phones on the separate sides of the plexiglass, "Hey, baby," Diva said, looking Roman in his eyes. The sight of her man made her moist between the legs, and his voice made her wetter. Roman, himself, had a hard-on. Everything about Diva was a turn on to him.

"I miss the shit outta you, wifey."

"Aaawwl, I miss you too."

"Hey yo, did you go holla at the dude about the parking lot fo' the rental car shit?"

"Nope, not yet."

"Maaan, what the fuck," Roman's face twisted up. Just that quick his dick went limp. People bullshitting when it came to business was a complete turn-off to him. He had been trying to have Diva take care of this business for like a month, and he was fed up with her stalling.

"Don't start, Roman."

"What the fuck you mean don't start. Who the fuck is you talkin' to?!" Diva didn't answer Roman, she just stared at him and hoped that he would calm down. She knew how quick-tempered he was, and how he could raise his voice to embarrass her.

"WHO THE FUCK IS YOU TALKIN' TO?! Y'all ma'fuckas think cause I got ten years y'all ma'fuckas can just do whatever, just talk to me like I'm soft, an' shit!"

"Don't nobody think you soft, Roman. And what do you mean y'all ma'fuckas?"

"You heard me y'all ma'fuckas,' Roman repeated himself, and paused, "When the fuck is you gon' take care of that business. I'm try'na put this shit together fo' ya dumb ass. When the Feds come asking how the fuck you got all that ice, money, cars, and all that shit, and ya ass can't explain that shit you goin' the fuck to jail. Stupid ma'fucka!"

Listening to Roman, tears began to stream down Diva's pretty face. Her eyes shifted side-to-side, she knew that people could hear him cursing her out. Just like that the visit that was supposed to be a joyous one was fucked Up. She had got dressed thinking about looking good for her man and going there to uplift him, and now the man that she loved with all her heart was belittling her, and talking to her like she was some dumb nigga off the streets.

"There's been a lot goin' on, Roman," she said trying to explain why she still hadn't taken care of the business he wanted her to take care of.

"Like what you smokin', hangin' out on some bullshit, not taken care of shit, being lazy, an' shit!"

"Roman, baby, please calm down. you're making a scene."

"Fuck all that. What the fuck was goin' on?!"

"That nigga Grinch beat 'Vette half to death, Ewee got killed, and I think Dice had some'in' to do wit' it, I don't know. Shit's just been crazy. And I'm not out here just gettin' high, and I'm not lazy! So, quit talkin' to me like that. I'ma take care of that business trust me, but you need to quit talkin' to me like I'm some random ass chick!"

"BITCH, YOU BULLSHITTIN'! I ain't try'na hear that shit!!"

"BITCH?! !"

"Yeah, you heard me, BITCH!"

SLAM!

Diva slammed the phone down, and hung it up, "Bye, Roman, Bye!" She said through the plexiglass. Roman couldn't hear her, but he could read her lips.

Our Love Is A Life Sentence

"Diva, pick the ma'fuckin' phone up...Diva!" Roman called out, but his words fell on deaf ears. Diva never even looked back, "He's not gonna talk to me like that, disrespect, an' shit. With all that I'm out here doin'," Diva mumbled to herself, wiping the tears from her face, terminating their visit, and leaving the prison. Roman had to sit there for the next forty-five minutes and think about how he had over-reacted.

"Fuck! Fuck! Fuck!" He said to himself, knowing that he had fucked up, and hurt Diva.

Forty-five minutes later he was back on the block, trying to call her, but she didn't answer. On her way back to Pittsburgh she cried hard and sobbed. She seen Roman calling, but she didn't have no rap for him at that point.

"Man, I fucked up!" Roman told Smooth inside of their cell during the afternoon count.

"What you meeeaan, bro?" Smooth said, looking over his bunk.

"Man, Diva, walked out of the visit on me."

"Yeeaah?!" This was what Smooth was trying to hear, "Maybe there is a chance of me fuckin' that bad ass bitch of this lame's," he thought to himself.

"Yeah. I been try'na have hear holla at this cat about this car lot, you know I was talkin' bout that rental car shit?"

Our Love Is A Life Sentence

"Yeah, yup."

"Well, I been try'na get her to get it' him, and put eh' thang together, but she been bullshittin, an' shit, you know?"

"And man, shit just got heated, an' I went the fuck off, and she just got up, an' walked off on me, ha," Roman said, with a chuckle.

"Damn, that's crazy, hm," Smooth said, with a sinister smile on his face, silently rubbing his hands together like he was about to go on a feast.

"Now she ain't answerin' the phone, an' shit."

"Mm mm mm. So, what you gon' do?"

"What you mean? I just gotta wait till she calms down, and talk to her you know."

"Bro, you doin' too much time to be stressin', you know? Why she says she haven't handled that business, yet?"

"She was sayin' some bitch we know got fucked up by dis nigga Grinch, an' she thinks my man was behind my man Ewee's murda, but she wasn't sure. You know she don't really be knowin' what be goin' on, you know?!"

"Who, the homie you were tellin' me about the other day. Why would ya man murk ya homie, tho?"

"I don't know? We ain't even get to get into all that."

"Well, look, fam', if you want me to ... If I get out on bail tomorrow, I can handle that fo' you, you know."

"Aw, that'll be wassup."

"Yeah, then she ain't gotta be worry 'bout it, an' you ain't gotta stress about it, you know."

"I could have my man do it, but he be wrapped up in other shit. So I don't be try'na, you know, put all that type of shit on him." "Bro, I got you. If they let me out."

"That'll be wassup," Roman said, leaning back on to the wall on his bunk.

Smooth was reminded that night that he had court in the morning. Him and Roman stayed up smoking exotic and blowing the smoke into the toilet as they flushed it repeatedly. Trying to killed the smell of the potent buds. Now after being processed, cuffed and shackled he was on his way to Federal. court. Where he would be debriefed, and maybe let go on bail. Whatever information he had to provide, he was willing to provide. He had even considered telling the Feds about Roman getting drugs into the high-security prison, but he decided that he would at that moment. He didn't want the Fed's having guards search his cell right after he went to court. That would be a dead giving. Everyone would know that he was working with the Fed's. He didn't want to raise any suspicion. He didn't want Roman to be alarmed in any way. But other than that,

Smooth, was willing to tell it all. Seeing banks come back reminded him that them making bail was all on the Feds. Apparently, Banks refused to cooperate and was sent back to Ohio to sit until trial.

AT THE FEDERAL COURT HOUSE, Smooth only sat in the holding cell for several minutes. Then he was lead into a conference room. He joined by his lawyer, Judas Rubenstein, two DEA agents working his case, and the United States District Attorney, Mary Goldberg.

"How you doing Mr. Farrier? I'm agent Martin Dunbar, this is my partner, Arthur Galloway."

There was a brief pause as the two made eye contact.

"I'm US Attorney, Mary Goldberg."

The agent and the US Attorney introduced themselves. The US Attorney cut the agent off and took charge.

"Have a seat," Smooth's attorney told him.

"Before I say shit, am I gettin' bail?!" Smooth asked.

"That's totally up to you. You give us some good information that we can use to convict members of your conspiracy known and unknown, and you can walk out of here today. Otherwise, you'll be stuck in prison until trial, more and likely, even likely, even longer. We have a 98% conviction rate," The DA told Smooth, dangling her deadly carrot over Smooth's head.

"What you want to know?" Smooth asked.

"Tell us about your celly, Roman Edmonds," agent Dunbar said. He to be in his early thirties, but his mostly silver hair gave away his older age.

"My celly?!" How the fuck they know who my celly is?" Smooth thought to himself. "What y'all wanna know about him?" He said, with his head cocked sideways.

Since you've been his celly has he been involved in any illegal activity that you know of?" Agent Dunbar asked, studying the puzzled expression on Smooth's face. He knew the answer to his question, he just wanted to see how honest Smooth was gonna be.

"Yeah, he got some drugs into the prison somehow. I don't know how, though," Smooth told agent Dunbar.

"Be honest. That's the only way this is going to work for you," Smooth's attorney told him.

"You didn't asked him how?" Agent Galloway asked, rearing his head back.

"Nah man! You don't ask questions like that," Smooth said, feeling offended by the lack of street sense the agents really had. They always acted like they were so street smart, but the truth was they only knew what the streets told them.

"Has he offered you any drugs to sell?" Agent Dunbar asked.

"No, but he told me if I got out he may have a homie that could put me on my feet," Smooth told the agent.

"Hold up, so he still got drugs on the streets?" Agent Dunbar asked, wondering how they missed the detail.

"Not that I know of. he just said he might have a hook up fo' me," Smooth answered.

"That's enough to get him on another conspiracy charge. This time we'll be able to career him and give him at least 240 months. Mr. Farrier, if we let you out on bail would you be willing to work with us to put this scumbag away for even longer?" The DA asked. She wanted Smooth to help put Roman away for at least another twenty years.

"If y'all let me out today, yeah, I will," Smooth said, agreeing to put a man that looked out for him away for two more decades.

"There's something else. I don't know if y'all can use it, but not long ago, ah couple days ago some bailer named Ewee got killed. Roman wasn't sure, but he believed that his man had killed him."

"Whoa, whoa, whoa, whoa, Mr. Farrier, you're telling me that the guy he's linking you up with killed someone?!" The DA stood up as she asked the question. Smooth knew he had their attention now, and that he would be out on bail in no time. "I don't know if it's the nigga he hookin' me up wit' or not, it might be. I'll hav' tah get out to see," Smooth said.

"Well, once you get out you're going to have to find this out right away, and let us know," agent Galloway said.

Our Love Is A Life Sentence

"If we can link Edmonds to this guy, it'll be a life sentence for both," the DA said, looking at the agents, and Smooth's lawyer.

Hearing this Smooth wished he didn't say anything about the shooting. He wanted to get out of jail, maybe even sacrifice a few people he really didn't fuck with, but a life sentence, he wasn't trying to put nobody away for life.

"Will I have to do anytime if I help y'all get Roman?" Smooth asked, realizing how valuable the information about the shooting was to the government officials.

"What we'll do is get you out on bail, and write you a 5K1 letter for you," the DA told Smooth.

"What will that do?" Smooth asked, wanted to know what he was agreeing to.

"Make you eligible for a huge time reduction. With you helping us with both conspiracies you'll probably walk scot-free," the DA told Smooth, putting a smile on Smooth's face.

"But you're going to have to fully cooperate with us. Wear a wire, do some controlled buys, and report everything that Edmonds tells you," agent Dunbar told Smooth.

"No problem. That's nothin'. Long as I ain't gotta do no time, an' shit," Smooth said.

"Yeah, get close to him, and whenever you hook up with his man call one of us, and we'll let you know how you could assist us," the DA said.

"Now, as far as your case," agent Galloway said, opening a manila envelope with Smooth's case file in it.

THREE HOURS LATER, the debriefing came to an end. The agents and the DA was more than satisfied with the information Smooth provided. He confirmed a lot of things that his co-defendants told them He also told them things about Banks that they didn't know. After the agents and the DA met with the judge and told him about the debriefing, he agreed to have a mock detention hearing. Which meant that there would be an argument between the DA and Smooth's lawyer, but regardless of what was said, Smooth would walk.

INSIDE OF THE COURTROOM, "This is the matter of Mr. Farrier here for the purpose of a detention hearing as I understand it. Is the government ready?" The judge asked, addressing the matter to the court.

THE DA: "Yes, your honor, thank you."

THE JUDGE: "Thank you."

THE DA: "Your Honor, really what we have here, as we typically done in this district if it's okay with the court, what's relevant to Mr. Farrier's situation is within the pretrial services report. What we have here is Mr. Farrier, a Federal Grand Jury returned a three-count indictment, it names Mr. Farrier as a co-conspirator of a very large cocaine distribution conspiracy. It charges that the conspiracy was responsible for at least five kilograms or more of cocaine.

Mr. farrier would be facing a mandatory minimum of ten years if convicted of his pending charges, along with this case. With a prior felony drug trafficking conviction, the potential exposure would be a mandatory minimum sentence of ten years, a very significant penalty, to say the least, he would be facing.

The government also notes the presumption for detention that is present in this case pursuant to stature. We also point out the fact that pretrial services has done a rather extensive investigation and report. Pretrial services is recommending detention in this case. The pretrial service office noted that they believe there are no conditions that could be imposed that would minimize the risk of danger to the community. So, based on the evidence from the Grand Jury and report from Pretrial Services, the government believes that those things warrant a finding of detention, your Honor."

THE JUDGE: "THANK YOU. Does the defense care to cross examine the Pretrial Service officer?"

DEFENSE ATTORNEY: "No, your Honor. Just make an argument based on what the DA has presented to the Court from the Grand Jury."

THE JUDGE: "Proceed."

DEFENSE ATTORNEY: "I certainly understand the presumption for defense given the nature of the charges and we do not disagree given the nature of the charges but it is a rebuttable presumption. Your Honor, I would also like to note in the Pretrial Service Report, the Pretrial Services department has investigated my client's girlfriend, who is present here in the courtroom, and it has noted that she agreed to provide a home for the defendant and they found her to be a suitable third-party candidate.

Therefore, he has a residence available to him if released on bond. He does have a pending case but has attended every court hearing to date, and I believe that is a plus. Pretrial Services even feels that condition could be fashioned to reduce the defendant's risk of nonappearance, which has never happened, may I add again.

So, I would submit the issue of appearance versus non-appearance was addressed within the four corners of this report and that Pretrial Services does, in fact, feel that appearance or non-appearance isn't the issue.

Now, assessment of danger is not an issue because my client does not have any criminal history of violence. In saying that, I would like to move on my client being a flight risk. A review of said defendant's record does not prove that he is a flight risk as the defendant is a life-long resident of Allegheny County, has no resources to leave the area, haves family members in the area and local ties to the community. Therefore, on behave on my client, I'm requesting that he be released on home confinement at least pending trial. With the information that now exist which overcomes the presumptions on which the government surely relies to keep the defendant incarcerated," hearing his lawyer's argument, Smooth, realized that he had been played.

He had sat for over three hours giving the Feds everything to build a strong case on his friends to make bail, and he didn't have to. He couldn't have made bail without saying shit.

THE DA: "You Honor, just briefly. I think something we sometimes forget is with respect to the issue of danger to the community, the courts have recognized that drug trafficking is a danger to the community in considering this under the Bail Reform Act. It's not strictly physical violence, but the danger to the community includes drug trafficking. In this case, this is very large drug trafficking with the highest quantities here being indicted."

THE JUDGE: "Thank you, sir," The judge said to the DA. "It's noticed, as the defense mentions, that thills gentleman is a lifelong resident of the area. We do have a presumption and the probable cause finding of the Grand Jury notes, some weight of evidence regarding the matter, but also think it's somewhat significant that the fact that the defendant has not been convicted of any crime yet says a lot.

There has not been crimes of violence nor previous drug offenses. But as far as the presumption, I think I would totally agree with

the defense. The presumption coupled with the things I just mentioned I think are enough to overcome and rebut resumption. For that reason, I am ordering that the defendant is no longer detained, and is released to his girlfriend's house on home confinement pending trial.

BAP-BAP! BAP-BAP!

The judge ordered, slamming his gavel down.

BY 8:00 pm, that night, it was clear to Roman and others that Smooth had made bond, and wasn't coming back. After a few unanswered attempts to contact Diva, she finally answered at 8:45 pm, "Hey, I'm at Ewee's wake, call me later," Diva told Roman in a whisper.

'Wight. Hey ... I love you, and I'm sorry."

"Kay, love you. Call me back."

Love you, too," Roman said, watching Big Stan go into his cell as he hung up the phone.

INSIDE OF HIS CELL, Big Stan flopped down on his bunk and picked up a letter that sat on his bed. It was a letter from his baby-mama, in it she was telling him how hard life was without him, and how much she needed his help to take care of their child. He wanted to open the letter and read it again, but it hurt him too much too. He was down bad. She was the only one coming through for him, and now she was complaining about how rough things were. Around the pod he made a few little moves, just enough to eat at night, but Roman and his boys had things on lock there. In his mind, he wished he wouldn't have played himself with Roman. Watching him, he realized like everyone else, that Roman was a real ass dude. As Big Stan contemplated, he noticed a shadowy-figure standing in his cell's doorway with something in his hand. It was Roman, holding a gray plastic property container, "What up, Big Stan?" Roman asked, standing in the doorway.

"What up, yo?!" Big Stan asked with his heart racing.

"I got a lil some'in' fo' you. I'ma be outta here soon. I might leave tonight, I don't know. But I wanna look out fo' you. I know how shit be, you know?"

"What you mean look out?"

"Here go some commissary fo' you, and..." Roman said, sitting the container down on Big Stan's cell floor, "...Here go a lil some'in' to get you right," Roman finished saying, extending a quarter of exotic to Big Stan.

"Damn fam', why you doin' dis?" Big Stan said, taking the bud from Roman. He couldn't believe what was taking place. He was just there stressing about his current situation, and now a blessing, if you would call it that, was being dropped at his doorstep.

"Like I said, I know how hard shit could be in this ma'fucka, you know. And I'm about to be out, so I wanted to spread some love around the unit before I dipped. Look, my lil homies might need you to do a lil collecting, an' shit, but that's up to you."

"Oh, ain't no problem. I got 'em, yo!"

"COUNT TIME... COUNT TIME!" The guard called out over the PA system. 'A'ight, they gon' let you know what's up. Put you down wit' shit."

"Maaan good lookin', Roman. You's ah real nigga," Big Stan said, shaking Roman's hand and embracing him. But he wasn't just saying that because what Roman was doing for what Roman was doing for him right then. He had heard about Roman standing up on his case, and everybody in jail recognized that as some real shit.

"No problem, homie," Roman said, leaving Big Stan's cell to go to his cell. Walking the tier he felt good about the man he was. He knew looking out for Big Stan was the right thing to do. Yes, they had beef, but that beef was handled and forgotten about as far as Roman was concerned. Now, he was making an ally out of what man would still consider an enemy. It was hood politics at it best.

SLLLAAAM!

Roman pulled his cell door shut. Looking out his cell's window, he looked at what he was confined to, and shook his head.

CHAPTER 14 CROSS THE DOUBLE-CROSSER

Walking out of the Federal court house a free man, Smooth, kissed and hugged his girlfriend, Kylie Pollard. "I'm so glad they let ya ass go!" She said, holding Smooth.
"Shit! You?! Me too," Smooth said, feeling as though he was given a second chance at life. Him not doing any time sounded even better than him getting out on bail, but he wasn't going to tell his girl about that. If he did he would have to tell her about him snitching, and she hated snitches. A snitch had put her mother in jail for fifteen years. So she despised a rat, and would definitely cut him off if she found out that he was working for the Feds. At that point, he didn't have anywhere else to go, so he definitely wasn't telling her that. According to Roman, he would have at least a couple years before his homies would know that he snitched on them. And if they all pleaded out they would never know because his statements would be sealed in what the court's called Jencks material. Jencks material was based on the case Jencks v. United States, 353 U.S. 657, 77 S. Ct. This material was obtained during pretrial discovery.

Discoverable statements including witness's signed or adopted written statements, and transcripts or recordings of a witness's oral statements, including grand-jury testimony. Along with the information Smooth gave, he also agreed to testify in front of a grand jury if the government needed him to.

Knowing what he knew he would tell his homies that the Feds revealed to him what they had, and advise them to plead out so that he would never be exposed as the rat that he was. Until then he was out with a license to ball, and a 'get out of jail free card. The Pretrial Service Office would be coming; to his girl's in the morning. They would be there to put an ankle monitor on his leg to track his every movement. On house arrest, it would be hard for him to make his move on Roman's girl, Diva. Because the Feds would be all over him. So that night would be the perfect time for him to move on her. And if he did it between nine and eleven O'clock, Roman, wouldn't be able to block the move. Because he called Diva around eleven-thirty every night. Besides that, no one would expect him to do something that risky his first night out on bail. If everything went as planned he would be able to look out for Banks, and make up for crossing him and their money getting crew. Banks was the only one he really cared about, but he had sacrificed him for bail as well.

Our Love Is A Life Sentence

AT SOUTHSIDE TATTOO'S, A Tattoo artist wiped down his work, "Is that cool?" He asked Bigga Figga.

"Hell yeah," Bigga Figga replied, checking out Ewee's name inked on his trigger finger. He would use it to kill the ones responsible for taking his cousin away.

After Bigga Figga and several of his goons got tatted in remembrance of their boss man's late cousin, they headed to a airbrushing shop a few doors down from the tattoo parlor. They went to pick up airbrushed hoodies they were going to wear to the wake and funeral service.

"Ewww shit! Check dis ma'fucka out, my nigga!" Bigga Figg4 said, holding up a 6x hoodie with a large picture of Ewee's face on the back of it. There were also the words: 'Life's A Gift, Death's A Promise,' over and under an exact rendering of his cousin's face. Only Bigga Figga and Timbo had got Ewee's picture down on their hoodies, others just got the words: 'R.I. P Ewee on their t-shirts. Only because the wake was that night and the airbrush artist wouldn't have been able to airbrush Ewee's face on everybody's hoodie in time.

"Anybody heard from dat nigga Grinch, yet?" Bigga Figga asked Timbo.

"Nah, not yet. Still haven't heard or seen dat nigga, bro."

Our Love Is A Life Sentence

Timbo said to Bigga Figga as they walked out of the airbrushing shop with their small entourage of goons behind them, carrying bags of rest in peace tee's.

"You locate his B.M?" Bigga Figga asked.

"Should have her address by tonight," Timbo told his street boss.

"Make sure you do. I don't care how much you gotta pay fo' it,

get dat shit!" "No doubt!"

"It's time to deal wit' dis shit, fam'."

ON THE WESTSIDE, Blonde, Dice and Evette met up at the transport spot. The girls needed to re-up. "This is it until we make another move," Dice told them, handing each of them a bag of logs. Over eighty racks in knots and rubber band-bundles covered the living room table. "Which one of y'all is gon': make that trip, this time?" Dice asked, patting his pockets for a Lighter to light up the dangling Newport hanging from his mouth.

"I'll make dat move, 'Vette's too banged up to," Blonde said, flickering her lighter to ignite the end of Dice's cigarette "Bitch, roll up. Let's smoke some'in. All dis ma'fuckin' bud in dis bitch," she said to Evette.

"Aight, I'll make the call tonight. Set that shit up fo' you to make that move inah couple days," Dice said, puffing on his cancer-stick, and blowing its deadly fumes into the air.

"Ewee's wake is tonight. We goin'?" Evette asked, pulling out a small zip-bag of buds from her Givenchy-pen book bag.

"I ain't try'na go over dat ma'fucka. I hate goin' to shit like that," Dice said, blowing more smoke into the air.

"So, if I die you ain't gon' come to my shit," Evette said, licking the wrap-paper, and tightly rolling up the blunt.

"Come on, man. You family, you my bitch. Look at all the shit

Our Love Is A Life Sentence

I'm goin' through right now fo' ya ass. You know I'ma represent!" "We should go. If we don't Bigga Figga is gon' look at it like we disrespectin' his fam'. Especially since y'all had dat lil pow-wow," Blonde said, watching Evette light up the blunt. "I already told that nigga I wasn't comin', an' shit," Dice said, with his head cocked sideways, looking at Blonde. "All I'm sayin' is we should go," Blonde said, looking back at Dice.

"Yeah, aight," Dice said in a irritated tone of voice. "What's the word on dat nigga Grinch. I haven't heard shit have y'all?" Evette asked, inhaling, and exhaling blunt smoke. "He might show up at the wake tonight," Blonde said. "If he does it's gon' be all bad fo' dat ass. Fuck dat wake," Evette said, still angry about what Grinch had done to her pretty face. She would be permanently scarred for life because of him.

"Naaah 'Vette, we can't do no shit like that, but we definitely need to get at that nigga. And I found out about a spot on the East where he be at. Maybe we should pay that nigga ah lil visit after the wake," Dice said.

"What, you tracked dat nigga down?" Evette asked.

"Yeah, but since then I can't pick up a trail on him." Dice said. "Somehow, he must of figured out he was being tracked," Blonde replied.

"But how, how would he know?" Dice questioned.

"You ain't sneak over there, and try to get at him without tellin' us, did you, Dice?" Blonde asked with a smile on her face. Putting a chain of blunt smoke in the air.

"Nah, but I sent the police over that bitch. They might have him. Nah, if they did it would've been on the news," Dice thought to himself. "Nah, but I did go over to check the spot out," he told the girls.

"Where's the house at?" Blonde asked Dice.

"Stanton Heights," Dice told her.

"I think dat's where his B.M. live at, dat's what I hear. But he might have just got rid of the phone. Eh'body know you can track them iPhones," Evette added.

"If that's where she's at then that's where he's at. And he might of caught on to the phone. Somebody might of put him up on game, but either way we gotta catch up wit' that nigga before Bigga Figga an' his goons do. So, if he don't show up at the wake, we over that bitch tonight," Dice said.

"Shit if he figured out that you tracked him there he might be on the move," Evette said, rolling up another blunt.

"If he ain't there, I'ma get him there," Dice responded.

211

"How you gon' do dat," Blonde asked as her and Evette looked at Dice.

"Y'all just leave that to me. I got this ... Let me hit that," Dice said, reaching for the blunt Blonde was smoking.

Our Love Is A Life Sentence

AT THE ALLEGHENY COUNTY Northshore precinct, "Jus were all over the apartment:
"Our perp', Lucas "Grinch" Sanford's," Detective Tomkins answered, ice chair to face his partner.spinning around in his chair to face his partner.
"You got it!" Detective, "Still doesn't prove shit the homicide. They were si he kill his friend knowin sense," Detective Tomkins the ordeal.
Y HOMICIDE AND ROBBERY DIVISION, at the got the prints back, and guess who's prints t?" Detective Gnocchi asked his partner.
The females put him there the night of, supposed to be hookin' up, remember. Why would
they were on the way? Doesn't make any said, trying to find some logic out of

CHAPTER 15 WAKE OF DEMISE

Ewee's murder hit Bigga Figga like a strike of lightning sent straight from God himself. Melancholy had set his gloomy-mood for days. Without the answers to his questions about his cousin's death, he couldn't eat or sleep. Stress along with the effect of the pills he was popping had thrown him into a depressive state of being.

Their family sought the help of local homicide detectives, on the other hand, he had put out his own manhunt for Grinch, the only person that he felt could answer his questions. But no one had heard anything from him, and this made Bigga Figga's suspicions of his cousin's friend grow to deadly lengths.

Running out of patience he was ready to take desperate measures and his hunt to another level. Through methods of kidnapping, torture or murder, he was willing to do whatever it took to find out what exactly happened the night of his cousin's demise.

Our Love Is A Life Sentence

AT THE WAKE, Bigga Figga had stood at his dead cousin's white and gold casket for over an hour. Watching his shoulders bounce from uncontrollable sobbing, several of his stiffened goons including, Timbo, stood at his sides war ready in black hoods as he cried a river of memories and vengeful thoughts. He thought about how great of a man Ewee was, "His lil man'll neva worry 'bout shit!" He said during a lengthy conversation with himself, thinking about his cousin's son and baby mama. The last image of Ewee was from his visit to the morgue. Closing his eyes, he tried to tune out the other outburst of cries from mourners, and focus on his cousin's face. As it appeared he flinched and shook his head, but he couldn't shake the vision of Ewee's disfigured face.

At the other side of the room, Blonde, Diva, and Evette, watched as Dice walked up to Bigga Figga to pay his respects. Throughout the room, there were sobs and stories of the fallen soldier that had brought the hood to a standstill. There was a long line of family and friends waiting to pay homage to the deceased weed man that laid dormant in the casket before them. Some would give their last words, others would place their hand on the coffin, speak their peace in silent and keep it moving.

"Wow, look y'all," Diva said to Blonde and Evette, pointing to a huge monitor that displayed photographs of Ewee from the cradle to the grave.

Dice gave half-smiles to onlookers in the long line as he bypassed them to get to Bigga Figga. Seeing the giant hood star with his head down, Dice, affectionately place a comforting hand on his shoulder.

Slowly shifting his head to his right side, Bigga Figga, smiled when he saw the one consoling him was Dice, "Thanks fo' comin', fam'," he said, placing his large mitt over Dice's hand.

"Wouldn't missed it fo' the world. Blonde, Diva and 'Vette's here too," Dice said.

"Dat's what's up," Bigga Figga mumbled.

"Anything you need just let me know, big fella, you heard?"

"Yeah yup," Bigga Figga said with a nod, turning his head back to Ewee's casket.

We gon miss you lil homie. You were ah real one," Dice said as he reached out his hand to touch Ewee's casket. Bigga Figga watched as Dice drew his hand back with teary-eyes. Then just as sudden as Dice appeared he was gone.

"You still want us to get dat nigga," Timbo, Bigga Figga's street capo asked.

"Nah, dat nigga ain't have shit to do wit' it, dig. Did you get Grinch's BM's address yet?" Bigga Figga asked Timbo.

"We'll have it soon as dis bitch show up. Matter of fact, let me.

"…Hey, here you go," a female said, handing Timbo Grinch's BM's address.

"Good look. Here," Timbo said, discreetly handing the female a stack as he hugged her.

"Got it, bro. We ridin' tonight?" Timbo said, asking Bigga Figga if they were going to seek vengeance on the grievous night of Ewee's wake.

"Hell yeah. In about a half. Let the homies know. Me and you gon' ride though. Too many cars, too many niggas ah get us pulled over fo' sho. You know how hot the Eastside be. And while we take care of dat have the lil homies go to the spot.an' turn all the way up fo' Ewee, feel me?" Bigga Figga told Timbo.

"Fo' sho, I'm ready, big bro."

ON THE EASTSIDE, Smooth walked out of an A-Plus convenience store with a small bag of Backwoods and goodies. After dialing a number on his cell phone, he put it to his. Ear and listened to it ring a few times before someone answered.

Nnnn nnnn nnnn.

At the wake, Diva, looked at the number displayed on her LCD screen as her cell phone vibrated and flashed, "Hello?!" She answered, walking out of the room Ewee's wake was being held in into the hallway.

"Is dis Diva?" Smooth asked, placing his bag of groceries on the top of his car, then leaning and resting his back against its door.

"Yeah, who's this?" Diva asked.

"My name is Tone. I'ma friend of Roman's. I got some money fo' him, and I was told to give it to you," Smooth lied, hiding his true identity.

"Well, I'm at ah wake right now. Can I call you right back?"

"Oh, I'm sorry to hear dat. Yeah, but um ... Make sure you call me right back tho'. I'm on my way outta town, and I need to get dis to you 'fo' I leave. I don't want Roman trippin', you know how he is."

"Ha ha, yeah. Might give me a minute and I'll hit you right back."

"Cool," Smooth said before hitting the end button on his cell phone.

"Who was dat, Bro?" Dice asked Diva, wondering if she was talking to Roman.

"I don't know. He said his name was Tone, and he got some money fo' Roman. But Roman never said anything to me about no Tone or no money," Diva told Dice.

"Me neither, and I know eh' body Roman knows, and I don't know Tone. We gon' hav'tah hit dat nigga back, an' see what the fuck he talkin' 'bout."

OUTSIDE, INSIDE OF DICE'S SUV, Blonde Dice and Evette listened as Diva called Smooth back, *Riiiinnng ... Riiinnng*

"Yo?!" Smooth answered after two rings.

"Yeah, this is Diva, Roman's woman. What you say ya name was?"

"Tone, I was up Ohio wit' Roman," Smooth said, "FUCK!" he also said in a whisper after revealing a part of who he really was. Now Diva knew that he was locked up with Roman, and if word got back to Roman he would know who Tone really was.

"Oh okay, you were locked up with Roman, huh?"

"Yeah, he looked out fo' me. I owe him some money and I was told to give it to you. I think he want you to put it towards that car rental place he tryna open. But like I said I'm about to leave town so I need to get it to you ASAP."

"Might, where you at now?"

"I'm on the East but I'm headed downtown. You wanna meet down there?" "Yeah, where at?"

"Meet me in the parking lot next to George Aiken's Chicken."

"Okay, I'll be there in like ten minutes," Diva told Smooth.

"Ask him how much money is it?" Dice whispered in Diva's ear.

"Hey, how much money is it?" Dice asked before Smooth could hang up.

"Twenty bands," Smooth said, lying again. He had four hundred dollar bills wrapped around the front and back of two-hundred-dollar bill stacks. He would use the two stacks as a diversion. His ultimate plan was to kidnap her and take her to her house to Rob her of Roman's stash.

"Okay, I'll see you when you get there. What kind of car you in?" Diva asked.

"Ah Black Altima."

"I'm in ah Navy Blue VW Atlas truck."

"Might cool. I'll see you when II get there … CLICK!" Smooth said before hanging up.

"Oh, dat's ah nigga Roman was locked up with' dat's why I don't know him," Dice said.

"But Roman never said nothin' to me about him or no money, tho'," Diva said.

"Shit don't sound right to me. Dat might be some shit Grinch is settin' up," 'Vette said.   I

"I mean but why would he try to set Diva up? Dat don't make no sense, I'm just saying," Blonde said.

"I don't know. Shit don't sound right, tho'. Look, hand me ya phone," Dice said, accepting Blonde's phone to put Grinch's BM's address in it, "I'ma follow Diva downtown

to meet dis nigga, y'all go over to dis address. It's Grinch's BM's spot. If dat nigga ain't
there, get him there, an' call me. I'ma head straight over dat bitch. We gon' end all dis shit tonight once and fo' all."

"Yeah, we need to. Dis shit's been draggin' on fo' too fuckin' long," Blonde said.

"Yea Big Bro, let's end dis shit. Tonight," Evette added.

Our Love Is A Life Sentence

BACK INSIDE OF THE WAKE, Bigga Figga was being held down by several of his dread-headed goon's. No longer able to hold his composure he screamed out, "I WANNA SEE. . .FUCK DAT! I WANNA SEE HIM! I NEED TO SEE HIM ONE MO' TIME!!" As he yelled he tried to pry open Ewee's casket. He didn't want the lasting image of Ewee's face to be a disfigured one. Before he could open it, Timbo, stopped him. Which made Bigga Figga flip out. "CALM DOWN! CALM DOWN! Calm down, bro," Timbo said as him and several homies wrestled Bigga Figga to the floor, "Hm... Hm ... Hm ... Hm, let's get outta here an' go handle dis shit. Just me and you, dawg," Timbo said in a. low tone of voice, and in between deep breaths.

"Mm hm, yea," Bigga Figga responded, nodding his head, "Somebody's paying fo' dis shit tonight, bro," He continued as Timbo helped him up.

OUTSIDE, three vehicles with Blonde, Dice, Diva, and Evette in them pulled away from the funeral home, and Grinch pulled up. Afraid to go inside he sat outside in his car. If the police wasn't looking for him he would have attended the wake and funeral.

"Damn Ewee Dawg, I'ma…Snst-snst, miss you, fam'," he said, crying. Then Bigga Figga and his dread-headed goon-squad came bursting out of the funeral home.

"What the fuck! Dat ain't good," Grinch said, slumping down in his seat as Bigga Figga and his goons loaded up into the vehicle's and skirted off.

CHAPTER 16 WRONG PLACES, WRONG TIMES

THE NIGHT OF EWEE'S WAKE, two detectives, two drive-by shooters, two lady hustlers, two Pittsburgh Police officer's, one kidnapper and his kidnap victim, and one street god's lives would be intertwined and altered. Some for the best and other's for the worse.

ON THE WAY DOWNTOWN PITTSBURGH,

Dice, ran a few scenario's across to Diva. He wanted to prepare her for whatever might happen. "Sis, 'member if he puts a gun to you just cooperate. Do whateva he tells you to do. Remain calm, and I'll make a move when the time's right," is one of the things Dice told Diva.

Diva's phone rang as her and Dice watched Smooth's Altima pulled into the dark parking lot. "Yeah," she answered.

"Yeah, I'm here," Smooth said.

"Yeah, I just seen you pull in. I'm walking' over to you now," Diva said, getting out of the truck. She was parked a few spaces down from Smooth.

As Diva walked to Smooth's car, Dice, slid over to the driver side of her truck and watched her every move. The tint on her truck's windows hid him from the sight of Smooth.

"Yooo, how you doin'? It's nice to finally meet you. You're all Roman talks about. Aaannd ... 1 don't mean any disrespect, but ya pictures don't do you any justice. You're mo' beautiful in person," Smooth said, trying to tear down the guard Diva had up. Then he popped his trunk, I got the money in my bag," Smooth said, reaching into his trunk.

"No Diva, walk away. It's a set up!" Dice said, knowing the game Smooth was playing. He was about to trunk her. Unfortunately for Diva was too far away to intervene. If he got out of her truck he would draw attention, and Smooth would have no other choice but react irrationally. So Dice's only option was to be patient, but Diva had other option's that he made her aware of.

"Here you go," Smooth said, handing Diva a bundle of money, "Dat's one of dem, aaaannnd here's ... BITCH, GET THE FUCK IN THE TRUNK!!" Smooth snapped, pulling a Sig Sauer .9mm out on Diva.

"Aaaggh!" Startled, Diva tried to back away from Smooth, but he grabbed her, "Don't turn dis shit into ah homicide! Pick that money up, and get'cha ass in dis trunk!" Smooth demanded.

Backing away from Smooth, made Smooth grab Diva up, and when he did, she dropped the money and her phone, it fell and slid under the car.

Pulling out of the parking lot, Smooth, activated the GPS on his phone. Its destination was to an address he got off a letter Diva sent to Roman. One day while Roman was on one of his weekly visits, Smooth, searched through his mail, and jotted it down.

Our Love Is A Life Sentence

Now at close proximity behind Smooth, Dice, watched as he approached a traffic light. A couple bar's away from it, Smooth, slowed down and then came to an halt.

"Come out, sis! Member what I told you," Dice said, with his hand tightly gripping a Smith & Wesson M&P Shield. Inside of the trunk, Diva, flicked her lighter aglow, and there it was, a Yellow tag that read, 'Pull in Case of Emergency.'

When Diva pulled the tag, the trunk popped open as Smooth ran Yellow light, turning Red. Him doing so caught the attention of police cruiser that came out of nowhere, "WHAT THE FUCK!" Dice, the police officer, and Smooth said in the same breath. Dice was shocked to see the police officer; the police officer was shocked to see Diva inside of Smooth's trunk, and Smooth was shocked to see his trunk open.

"WOOP-WOOP!" The policeman signaled his light's. This made Smooth hit the gas. The propulsion almost made the trunk shut close, and the acceleration forced Diva back further into the trunk.

"In pursuit of a Black Altima, tag number B-H-G 1220, with a possible kidnap victim in the trunk," said the officer over the radio.

Our Love Is A Life Sentence

ON THE EASTSIDE, detective's Gnocchi and Tompkins watched Ella's house from their parked car. They wanted to see if Grinch would show up before they knocked on the door this time. "I tell you what if this bastard doesn't show in the next twenty minutes we're going in that house," detective Gnocchi said.

"Hol', we got some action," detective Tompkins said. "Is that him?"

"No, it's a female."

"What the hell is she doin' coming from the side of the house?" Detective Gnocchi said.

KNOCK-KNOCK-KNOCK!

Evette knocked on Ella's door. Her and Blonde had parked around back. Before getting out of the car they argued about who was going to approach the house, "If he sees you at the door he ain't gon open it. You need to let me handle this," Blonde argued.

"If he comes to the door I'm shootin' through dat bitch! I got dis. You and Dice ain't gon' keep handlin' my business. Dat nigga fucked me up, not you. Not Dice!"

'Wight. Whateva, girl. Go 'head," Blonde said, giving into Evette, even though she knew that they were making the wrong move.

"Who opened the door?" Detective Gnocchi asked.

"Looks like the baby ma. Still no sign of our guy," detective Tompkins said.

With her back turned towards them, the two detectives couldn't see the Hi Point, Evette, was pointing at Ella, "Ssshhh, don't say shit! Just back in to the house," Evette said to Ella.

Opening the door without asking who was at it had put Ella in a bad predicament. She believed that she was opening the door for Grinch, but to her surprise, she was looking into the gun barrel and dark depths of a lady Scarface's eyes.

"Don't hurt us, please. I got kids here with me," Ella told Evette.

"You won't get hurt if you do exactly what I tell you to do. Is he here," Evette asked backing Ella into the house, and closing the door behind her. She could hear the kids playing upstairs in the house.

"Who is who here?" Ella acted clueless.

"She now, bitch, you gon' make me shoot you. Now, I'ma ask you one ma'fuckin' mo' time, 'is he here?!"

"No, Grinch is not here," Ella said followed by a loud sigh. She was sick of Grinch involving her and their kids in his bullshit.

'Wight, take dis phone. Call him and tell him, and get him over here," Evette murmured, throwing Ella a burn out phone.

"I have to get his number it's over there. He just gotta new phone," Ella said annoyingly honest, pointing to a piece of paper sitting on the living room table.

"Get it, but if you try some dumb shit I'ma empty dis clip in ya ass. So, don't play with me!"

"I'm not. I just need to get the number. Can I please ask you some'in", tho? What is this about?"

"You see these scar on my face, dis is what dis shit's about. Ya baby daddy tried to kill me, and he's gon' pay fo' dat shit tonight," Evette said, after a short pause. But deep inside she really didn't know what her next move was going to be. Her beef
was with Grinch and not his baby mama and their kids. Now that Ella had seen her face she didn't know what she was going to do. If she killed Grinch she would also have to kill Ella after revealing her face to her.

Ring-ling-ling-ling," Evette could hear the phone ringing in Ella's ear.

"Put it on speaker," Evette told Ella.

"CLICK! Ring-ling-ling. Yep! Grinch answered.

"Where you at?"

"On my way, there. I just came from Ew-Wee's wake," Grinch told Ella. "How far away are you?"

"Bout ten minutes away, why, wassup? You need some'in'?"

"Nah, I just wanna make sure you're

"Yea, bitch!" Evette said, with an approving nod of her head. "Whose phone number is dis?" Grinch asked, suddenly aware of the new number Ella was calling from.

"Mm mm. bitch!" Evette mock whispered, shaking her head, no, and pointing her Hi Point at Ella's head.

"When ,I went to Wal-Mart earlier I grabbed you a few burn outs, they were on sale for ten dollars. I know ya going to want to switch up," Ella said.

'Wight, I'll be there in ah minute," Grinch said before hanging up. Clinching his Glock 43, and hitting the gas. He knew that Ella and their kids were in trouble by the way she was talking. Only minutes away he mentally prepared himself. He was willing to die about his family.

"Okay, now what?" Ella asked.

"Sit down. Now I make my call and we wait," Evette said as she dialed Dice's number, and put the phone to her head.

"Yo?!" Dice answered.

"I'm here wit' Grinch's bm and he's on the way here. Where you at?"

"I'm at the NO. 2 Station."

"What?! What the fuck you doin' there?"

"I'm waiting on Diva. Dat crazy ma'fucka tried to kidnap her..."

"Whaaat?!" Evette responded, keeping her eyes and gun on Ella. "...Yea, then Diva popped the trunk from the inside...Ha ha, and the police was right behind 'em."

"Yo, dat's crrraaazy!"

"Hell yeah. She's cool, tho. They caught dude and booked him. They took Diva for questioning, she on her way out now. Soon as she come out, T we gon' shoot over there. Just keep 'em hostage 'til we get there."

"Nah, just tell me what to do. I can handle dis shit, bro."

"Look, dis how we gon' play dis, we gon' offer dude ah deal to get outta town and not come back..."

"No, uh-uh! Fuck no! Ain't no deal, bro. After all dis shit, you try'na offer him ah deal?!"

"Look 'Vette, by now the B.M. has seen ya face, and Grinch is on his way. When he gets there you only have one choice if you eliminate dis one, and that's to take 'em all out, the B.M., him and the kids, and I don't want dat on ya conscience, shit, I don't want dat on my conscience. Sis, I ain't try'na see you all mental, doin' life our worse over dis shit When I sent y'all over there I wasn't thinkin' straight.

We should have just laid on dude. We shouldn't have involve her and the kids."

"Yeah, you right."

"So, dis is what we gon' do, we gon' offer him some change, and tell him to leave the city. He gon' bite cause he's on the run anyway, and when shit cools down, and he's slips back into town, we gon' smoke him. Dat's if Bigga and his boys don't get to him first. We played our hand just right by goin' to the wake, and now all fingers point at him, you know?"

"Yeah, hell yeah."

"Aight, let me holla at her."

CLICK!

"You on loud speaker, bro," Evette said.

"Can you hear me?" Dice asked: Ella.

"Yeah, she can hear you. Bitch, answer him!"

"Yes, I hear you."

"Look, dis is what we know; We know Grinch is on the run from the police and Ewee's people. The way the streets tell is he robbed and killed homie. On top of dat, you see my people's face. You see what he did to her?"

"Mm hm," Ella responded, looking at Evette's face.

"Now, how could you be with ah man like dat. Dat beat up on beautiful women, and try to kill 'em..." Dice paused to let what he was saying sink into Ella's head. "...Now, you have a couple options here, you got 'A' and you got 'B'. A, is my people wait fo' Grinch to get there, and she starts shootin' until eh'body dead..."

"Uh-uh ... No, please!"

"Or B, around Twelve o' clock I get y'all fifty stacks, and Grinch leaves the 'Burgh fo' good. I never wanna see him again. Now, what you wanna do? The choice is all yours," Dice said.

"I choose 'B'."

"I knew you were a smart girl. You got ya'self out the hood, and ya try'na make a betta life fo' you and the kids. Now, it's up to you to convince Grinch it's in his best interest to never be seen again. You agree?"

"Yeah, I agree. I got you.

"...Mommy ... Mommy," Ella's kids ran down the steps calling her name.

"Y'all get over here, and sit down," Ella told her kids to have a seat on the couch.

OUTSIDE OF ELLA'S HOUSE, homicide detectives Gnocchi and Tompkins watched as a 2013 Hyundai Sonata CLS pulled up, and 'slow down in front of the house.

"Is that our guy," detective Gnocchi asked, before he seen the upper-half of a hooded body come out of the passenger side of the car.

INSIDE OF ELLA'S HOUSE, "Mommy, we're hungry," little Misty said. "Girl, just get ya ass over here and sit. I'll fix y'all some..."

THUMP-THUMP-THUMP, CRRRAAASSSH! THUMP-THUMP-THUMP, BURRRSSSHH!

OUTSIDE OF ELLA'S HOUSE, Timbo fired off rounds from a Draco with a 75-round drum on it, "THUMP-THUMP-THUMP... SCURRRRR!" Bigga Figga burned rubber and his wheels screeched as he pulled off. Started up the undercover vehicle detective Tompkins pulled off in pursuit as detective Gnocchi called in for back up, "This is detective Gnocchi I'm in pursuit of a dark colored Hyundai Sonata on Oranmore Street in Stanton Heights I'm requesting back, I NEED BACK UP!!"

INSIDE OF ELLA'S HOUSE, hearing the burst of gunfire Evette

dove into action and covered little Clay and Misty with her body. Gunshots shattered windows and a lamp in the living room. Her nostrils flared as she heaved heavily and her heart pumped adrenaline and fear.

"VETTE! VETTE!" Dice yelled into the phone.

"WHAT'S GOIN' ON, BRO! WHAT HAPPENED?!" Diva asked, getting into the waiting SUV. All into what he was hearing over his phone, Dice, failed to notice Diva walking out of the NO. 2 Station, and get into the truck.

"AAGGGHH...NOOOOO! PLEASE NO ... PLEASE NO!!" Ella cried out after the gunfire subsided. Hearing the gunfire and seeing glass shatter everywhere she dove to the floor for protection. Now she was praying to God that her kids were not killed.

"Vette, please answer me," Dice said into the phone after hearing Ella scream. He feared the worse.

Hearing Dice's voice, Evette, looked around for the phone, "AAAAH ...MOMMEEE ... AGH, MOMMY," Ella's kids cried. Evette had saved their lives,

"AH ... AH, yeah bro?!"Evette said into the phone. When she raised her body up from Ella's kids they ran to their mother's open arms, "Mommy, I'm scared."

"It's okay, Misty. Mommy got you.

"YOU GOOD?! WHAT THE FUCK HAPPENED?!" Dice asked.

"Yeah, I'm straight. I think dat was Bigga and his homies."

"Get the fuck outta there. Leave the bitch the phone, but you get the fuck outta there,

'Aight, I'm out. CLICK! Here," Evette said. After hanging up with Dice she threw Ella the cell phone, "They aight?!" She asked Ella.

"Mm hm, thank you," Ella said.

"We'll be in touch tomorrow jotting to the rear entrance."

"ELLA, YOU OKAY?!" Grinch questioned with his pistol in hand.

"THEY ARE DRAMATIZED ENOUGH!!" Ella said, holding their kids tightly.

"PUT THAT SHIT AWAY," knowing that if it wasn't for Evette acting fast her kids could have been dead.

"Do the right thing," Evette said.

"What happened?" Grinch asked.

"Somebody did ah drive-by on my house, and she saved us!"

"She, who?!"

"The chick with the scars on her face. The one you tried to kill. What the fuck is wrong with you, Lucas?!"

"PUT YA FUCKIN' HANDS UP! DON'T MOVE!!" An officer of the law said as he entered Ella's house. After calling for back up, detective Gnocchi, call for officers to check for survivors at Ella house, and to look for a fugitive on the run named, 'Lucas Sanford.'

CHAPTER 17 WICKED, THIS WAY COME

IN THE DOWNTOWN PITTSBURGH PARKING LOT, "Got it!" Dice said, reaching under a car for Diva's cell phone that got lost in the kidnapping.

"Thanks, bro. Damn, I missed Roman's calls," Diva said, checking her call log.

"Wait 'til he hears 'bout dis shit," Dice said.

"I know, right?! He's gonna lose his mind."

"Fuck yeah!"

"Mm mm mm, this has been one crazy night, a wake, a kidnapping and a drive-by shootin', and no wonder why look at the moon," Diva said, pointing up to the full moon that lit the summer sky. But what she didn't know was the action was not over with. Bigga Figga and Timbo's high-speed chase was about to come to an end.

HIGH-SPEED CHASE, "I ain't goin' back to jail, Timbo!" Bigga Figga said, calmly but meaningfully. "They gon' try to give us life especially if we killed somebody in dat house," he continued.

"I ain't doin' life, family. Fuck dat! Timbo said, shaking his head, no.

"We'll we mind's well go all out, then," Bigga Figga said, staring into his little homies eyes with a menacing, street-medicated glare.

"All out it is, family. Fuck the police!" Timbo said, staring back at his street god. He always claimed that he would die for Bigga Figga, and now, on this particular night, his death wish came calling.

"Yeah, fuck 'em, lil bro. I'll see you and Ewee in the next life, my nigga!" Bigga Figga said, looking back at the police cruiser's and flashing lights in his rearview.

"Hmph! Yea, if there's ah heaven fo' ah gangsta, big bro," Timbo said as he shifted his body around to position himself in a shooting-squat, "THUMP-BURRSSHHH-THUMP-THUMP-THUMP!" He let off a semi-automatic burst of gunfire that sent a police cruiser crashing to the side of the road, but there were others and more on the way. They knew as much and was prepared to die in a hail of gunfire.

"Play: 'Is There Ah Heaven Fo' A GANGSTA,' by Master P.," Bigga Figga said into his phone, and the song began, to play through the car speaker's.

"Rest in peace 2Pac," Master P. yelled out to 2Pac up in heaven, "DOOM-DOOM-DOOM-DOOM-DOOOM...DOOM-DOOM-DOOM-DOOM. Is there ah heaven fo' ah gangsta-gangsta-gaaangsta, ugggh! Is there ah heaven fo' ah gangsta-gangsta-gangsta, ugggh! Is there ah heaven fo' ah gangsta!" Bigga Figga and Timbo rapped the hook with Master P. They both loved the song, but on this night, it bred a new meaning and a different significance.

THUMP-THUMP-THUMP-THUMP!

Timbo continued to fire Draco rounds at those in pursuit of him and his big homie, including detective's Gnocchi and Tompkins. In the homicide detective's minds they believed that their night would be a regular night for cops and crooks, but it was turning out to be something far from that. Thrumming off more deafening gunfire, Bigga Figga and Timbo chimed the chorus with Master P, "IS THERE AH HEAVEN FO' AH GANGSTA-. GANGSTA-GAAANGSTA, UGGGH!" This time as loud as they could.

THUMP-THUMP-THUMP-THUMP, sung Timbo's AK-47 pistol as he sprayed at everyone and everything in the back of them.

"AAAAGH FUCK!" Bigga Figga wailed as a hot shell flew from the chamber of the Draco and went down his shirt, and singed his chest.

"OH SHIT!!!"

... CRASH...SKIRRRT. BOOOMP!!

Traveling at 90 miles per hour, Bigga Figga, was unable to stop. Losing control he tried to maneuver, and steer his car away from colliding into the rear, left side of a McDonald's tractor trailer, but couldn't.

A FEW MINUTES BEFORE, Evette ran out of the back door of Ella's house, and jumped into Blonde's waiting vehicle. Blonde skidded off, "What the fuck happened?!" She asked Evette, and then, "WOOP-WOOP!" out of nowhere several Pittsburgh police cruisers appeared in Blonde's rearview mirror. "Yo, what the fuck? Did you kill dat bitch?!" Blonde asked, contemplating whether she should pull over or not.

"No, I didn't kill nobody! I saved dat bitches kid's lives. Ma'fuckas did ah fuckin' drive-by while I was in dat bitch. Pull over," Evette said, dropping their gats to the floor, and kicking them under her seat with the back of her foot. But as Blonde was pulling to the side of the road, the police cruisers flew past them.

"Oh shit, dat was crazy. Should I turn around?" Blonde asked Evette.

"Nah, dat'll make us look hot. Just keep goin dis way," Evette replied.

THUMP-THUMP-THUMP-THUMP!

Timbo's Draco could be heard blocks away.

"Ew shit! Somebody's dumpin' like ah ma'fucka!" Evette said. "Dat's ah ma'fuckin' choppa. Dat's prolly Bigga an' dem niggas. They probably shot dat bitches spot up. Now, the po-po's on they ass," Blonde said.

"Look at dat shit!" Evette said, pointing to a shot-up police cruiser on the side of the road. Flashing his flashlight into their car, the officer waved them forward, and then,

CRASH ... SKURRRT... BOOMP!

They heard a crash.

"BIGGA FIGGA AND DEM!" Blonde and Evette said, simultaneously. "Bitch, look at all dem fuckin' cops," Blonde said.

Our Love Is A Life Sentence

AT THE SITE OF THE CRASH, 26-year-old, "Ronald Gasby," was the first to approach the 2013 Hyundai Sonata flipped on its side, that leaked a trail of gas.

"Ma'fuck da pop ... Ma'fuck da po-lice...Only God can judge me, " Bigga Figga mumble. Blood poured from his mouth. The crash had made him bite the tip of his tongue off.

Drawing his service weapon, officer Gasby, proceeded to approach the wreckage, and could partially see a heavy-set man that looked to be in his mid-thirties. When he came into Bigga Figga's view, two shots rung out, "POP-POP! Blowing him backward, off his feet.

The two shots were also heard by Blonde, Evette and the officer that waved them ahead, followed by a barrage of gunshots.

POP-POP POP. BOOM-BOOM! POP-POP-POP!

A total of 116 shots were fired.

Officer Gasby only heard the first shot right before it blew the top of his forehead and service hat off. Tearing through the rookies human life, and ending it.

Seeing their colleague shot dead in the street set off a deadly reaction, sixteen officers at the scene of the crash unloaded their weapon's.

"Damn, it's goin' down!" Blonde said as they drove closer to the wreckage.

Unable to respond to the shots that echoed from close proximity, the officer that waved Blonde and Evette forward, listened to the call of the dispatcher, "OFFICER DOWN-10-24-OFFICER DOWN!"

"Oh shit! Bitch, go-go!" Evette said as Blonde sped past the shooting.

"Oh, my dear is dat Timbo?!" Blonde asked. Seeing the police firing multiple shots into the Hyundai Sonata and Timbo's lifeless body made her put her hand to her mouth. The impact of the collision had sent him flying forward out of the rear windshield, killing him instantly.

"Yeah, dat's him, girl," Evette said, capturing Timbo's overkill on her cell, phone as Blonde drove pass.

Looking back through her driver-side mirror, Blonde, placed a call to Dice. Putting the phone to her face, it began to ring.

"Dat's fucked up......Dat's. fucked up ... They always kiln' us," Evette cried out.

"Yo babe, what up?" Dice answered.

"Babe, Timbo's dead, and I think Bigga is too!" Blonde said, with sadness in her voice.

Our Love Is A Life Sentence

"What you mean, what happened?!" Dice asked, sitting up in his car seat.

"They got into ah shoot-out with the police and crashed. We're driving..."

...BOOM... BOOM ... KA-BOOM!

Bigga Figga's car exploded, and blew a dozen officer's off their feet, including detective's Gnocchi and Tompkins.

"YOOO!!" Blonde bellowed.

"WHAT DA FUCK, YO?!!" Dice expressed, hearing the explosion in the background of their call.

"Shit's crazy, babe. Their car just exploded!" Blonde answered. "Sis, please get us da fuck outta here!" Evette said.

"Bro, what the fuck is goin' on?!" Diva asked, hearing all the excitement over the phone as they sat in her SUV in front of her house.

"Bigga Figga and Timbo just got killed in ah shoot-out with the police, and their car exploded an' shit. It's crazy out here tonight ...Yo, y'all hurry up and get back to the west. I don't need y'all gettin' caught up in dat shit." Dice said to Blonde.

'Wight, we on our way. Love you!"

"Love you, too."

ON THE SET IN HAYES MANOR PROJECTS,

"Sin-Dawg," Bigga Figga's third in command, and his homies celebrated Ewee's death. "Is This The End," from Rae Zellous Cook Up played as they partied in the street. Smoking, popping pills, drinking, pouring out liquor, and winding their Ewee Rest In Peace tee's in the air, all in honor of the fallen soldier.

Running out of her building, Syria, came out yelling, with tears streaming down her face, "SIN ... SIN ... YO, SIN?!" She ran up, and hugged Sin-Dawg.

"What up, sis? What's wrong?" Sin-Dawg asked, looking down at her in his arms.

"Bigga Figga and Timbo died in ah shoot-out with the 5-0 on Penn Aye, and they car blew up ... Snst..Snst," she said, looking up at Sin-Dawg.

"WHAT?! WHAT DA FUCK YOU TALKIN' 'BOUT?! MY NIGGA'S AIN'T DEAD!" Sin-Dawg said, in denial.

"My sister just called me and told. They seen it. They all was on the east.

Hearing that made Sin-Dawg come to reality. Hearing the Eastside made him know that it was real. He knew what they had planned to

do. "Yo, turn the music off! YO!!" The music stopped, "DA MA'FUCKIN' POLICE KILLED OUR HOMIES,

BIGGA AND TIMBO ON THE EASTSIDE. WE RIDIN' OVER DAT MA'FUCKA, LOAD UP!" He said as him and Syria got into his car, and pulled off.

CHAPTER 18 TRANSFER OF POWER

AT THE SCENE OF THE WRECKAGE, Sin Dawg and the rest of Bigga Figga's street thugs could barely get a glimpse of the aftermath the car explosion left behind. The three monstrous booms rocked Penn Avenue, caused store front windows to burst and shatter, set off car alarms and police officer's to be blown off their feet.

Fire Department Emergency Medical vehicles and ambulance's red and-white lights lit up the area. Paramedic's pulled out equipment-first aid kits and orange and white backboard's, to give assistance to those that sustained minor injuries from the car blast.

Shoving his way, through the crowd that gathered around, Sin Dawg, stood on his tip-toes to look over other spectator's for a glimpse of his street god. The sight of seeing the third of three-body bag's being zipped up, made him feel sick to his stomach, and his knee's buckle. Panic set in, and he froze, unable to say a word.

"What we gon' do, cuz?!" A low-level soldier of Bigga Figga's asked Sin Dawg before he responded. "We ain't gon' do shit! You see all these ma'fuckin' police, FBI Agent's and detectives around dis bitch. Matter-of-fact, we need to be out before these rna'fuckas start trippin' an' shit," Sin Dawg said.

"You serious, fam?! We ain't gon' ride on these ma'fuckas fo' what they did to Big Homie?!"

"Nigga, you crazy! Look, you can do whatever you wanna do, but I'm out. Come on, Syria," Sin Dawg said, fighting his way back through the crowd of spectators.

AT DIVA'S HOUSE, Diva held Diva as she cried, uncontrollably. "Shit gon' be a'ight, sis. Don't cry," Dice said, trying to comfort Diva. Too much had happened in one night, and her not being able to talk to Roman broke her down. "1 need Roman, bro. I want him home. I'll do anything to have him here with me. I'm tired of being alone and raising our son all by myself. They gave him ten fuckin' years, bro ..."

Snst, snst ...

"Somehow I gotta get him out. I just have to," Diva said with a shaky voice, and tears streaming down her beautiful face as her bottom-lip quivering as she spoke.

"You gon' be a'ight, sis, I swear. He ain't gon' do dat whole ten years. They got new law's coming out dat's gonna cut his time in half," Dice replied, staring into Diva's tearful eyes.

"Will you stay with me tonight, please," Diva pleaded, staring at Dice's juicy, plumped lips.

"Hmmm, sis ... Yea, I'll stay wit' you," Dice replied after thinking about it for a few seconds.

"Aww, thank you, bro. Come on, let's crack dis bottle of Hennesy an' smoke some'in'. I'm stressed the fuck out, bro," Diva said, leading Dice upstairs to her bedroom.

LATER THAT NIGHT AT 4:30 A.M., C.O. Orlando Dugan, read the early edition of the Post-Gazette as he sat at his station on B-Block. The front page showed a picture. Of the car accident that occurred on Penn Avenue: CAR EXPLOSION INJURES LAW ENFORCEMENT AGENCIES, KILLING THREE, Read the caption under the photograph. Bypassing everything else on the front page Officer Dugan's eye's locked in on the article that was linked to the picture:

ARTICLE ONE:

Two Sheridan men died Tuesday evening after striking the rear end of a McDonald's semi-tractor trailer. The incident took place shortly after 10:00 P.M., on Penn Avenue. According to police, two Allegheny County Homicide Detectives were conducting surveillance shortly before 10:00 P.M. last night when they observed two suspects in a dark colored Hyundai Sonata stopped in front of a home on Oranmore Street and mercilessly sprayed it with a barrage of gunfire ... CONTINUED Cl.

CONTINUED FROM Al:

When undercover Homicide Detective's attempted to stop the vehicle the driver Theartis Scott, 29, and his passenger Timothy Currington, 22, both of Pittsburgh, fled the scene and detectives initiated a pursuit. Other officer's in the area responded to shots fired. Activating their emergency lights, they also attempted to make a traffic stop. But the driver continued to flee at a high rate of 90 plus miles per hour North towards Penn Avenue.

Unable to stop, the incident surrendered when the driver lost. control of his vehicle and struck the rear end of a 2007 McDonald's semi-truck being driven by Emmit Macklin, 61, of Virginia. Upon contact the Hyundai Sonata rotated and then collided against a light post, and burst into flames before exploding.

Ejected from the rear of the vehicle, the passenger Currington was dislodged from the vehicle into the street of Penn Avenue. Currington was the first to die at the scene. After the crash, Allegheny Sheriff Officer, Doyle Van Dyke, 27, was involved in a shooting with the driver, Scott. While trying to rescue the driver in connection with the traffic fatality the rookie officer was shot twice and suffered from upper body injuries. Allegheny County Fire Rescue Medic's responded and transported Van Dyke to UPMC, where he died from his injuries.

After firing fatal shots into rookie officer Van Dyke, Scott also died at the scene. The driver of the McDonald's semi-truck suffered minor injuries and was the only survivor of the crash.

Allegedly Scott's collision with the semi caused his gas tank to leak and eventually explode, injuring at least a dozen officer's in which none sustained any life-ending injuries.

"Mm mm mm, these young ma'fuckas are crazy out here," C.O. Dugan said as he began to read another article. The heading read: DRIVE BY LEADS TO PERSON OF INTEREST:

ARTICLE TWO:

Last Monday evening, Allegheny Police Department received a 9-1-1 call shortly after 12:00 A.M. The caller stated that a man had been shot in his doorway. At 12:25 A.M. Allegheny Homicide Detective's reported that Donald "Ew-Wee" Portland, 28, of Sheridan answered the front door at his home on Zephyr Avenue after hearing a few knocks.

Deputies said several shots were fired, one fatally striking Portland once in the head. Based on preliminary information, police said the shooting does not appear to be a random act and they are still working to determine the identity of the suspects responsible for the shooting. During the course of the investigation, evidence was collected from Portland's home and was sent to the Pennsylvania Department of Law Enforcement's Crime Lab and lead investigators to Lucas Sanford, a person of interest, sought for questioning about the shooting. Through a combination of investigative leads and eye witness interviews, police learned that Sanford was there at the time of the shooting.

Now as a result of a drive by shooting, Allegheny County Sheriff's Officer's arrested Sanford on unrelated charges, after conducting a search at Stanton Heights home. And now, Sanford is being charged with possession of a firearm by a convicted felon, possession of ammunition by a convicted felon and violation of Federal Probation. According to investigator's no one inside of the residence was hurt by the drive by shooting that lead them to the suspect.

"Whoa, you couldn't make this shit up!" C.O. Dugan said, checking his watch. It was time to wake up the several inmates on his list that was getting transferred that morning.

INSIDE OF ROMAN'S CELL, Roman awoke when he heard his name being called over the cell intercom,

"EDMONDS… EDMONDS," Officer Dugan called out. After giving Roman instructions, Officer Dugan continued to alert the other inmates on his transfer-list. There were ten names in total.

Roman sat up in his bunk and started to mentally prepare himself for the transfer when he heard his cell door pop open, "Fuck...
Mm mm mm. It's finally time to leave dis bitch," he mumbled as he stood up Hearing his name called out other inmates went to their cell windows to get one final look at their big homie and bid him a farewell.

Roman had waiting two years for this moment to arrive. He felt nervous, a little, and sad at the same time. He had the butterflies and felt like he had to shit. This process would strip him of all his power. He had to leave everything and everyone behind, and start all over again., The only items that he would be able to take with him was his Bible and Legal work. All his commissary would be given away and the monies owed to him would be collected by his homies and sent to him.

Roman's drug operation would cease, but there would be someone else that would step up and take his place. How they would get their narcotics into the prison he didn't know and didn't care.

After Roman took a shit, he showered and took his commissary to Jarvis' cell. "Aight, bro," he said to Jarvis as he embraced him.

"Be safe, family. You got my info, stay in touch ... And um ... Don't worry 'bout dat guap., I got you, my nigga," Jarvis said. As Roman went back to his cell his other homies banged on their cell door's, "BE SAFE, RO-MAN ... GET AT ME, MY NIGGA ... LOVE YOU, BOY!" They yelled out. Roman saluted them, grab his box of property from his cell, and went to the bottom tier with the other convicts that were also being transferred.

Stepping out of the bubble, C.O. Dugan walked into the unit with a clipboard in hand, and began calling names. After their names were called and checked off, the convicts lined up in a single-file line at the Unit's entrance.

NNNN-CLICK!

The Unit door opened and the convicts followed another C.O. to R&D, where they were processed for transfer. Each convict was strip-searched, dressed into the clothes they were arrested in, and handcuffed. After being locked up for close to three years Roman's clothing were outdated and had a stale smell to them. Once everyone was searched and dress they were marched out of the back entrance of the prison. A transportation van and shotgun totting guards awaited their arrival. The guards reminded Roman of WWF wrestlers. The scene seemed to be straight out of a prison movie.

Our Love Is A Life Sentence

After being loaded into a white transfer van, they were driven to an Airport hanger, three hours away. Where other F.B.O.P transfer vehicles awaited. Convicts were being shuffled like cattle from van to bus or from van to the FBOP plane. It was at that moment that Roman realized how big of a business the prison system was.

Taken from the van to a large bus, Roman, was seated next to a heavily tattooed convict that looked to weigh approximately 280 pounds, solid. Taken his seat, Roman, solemnly nodded at the convict as he examined the tattoos on the convict's face. He made sure to do it without staring. The convict nodded upward but didn't bother to say a word. "Nigga think he hard, an' shit!" Roman thought to himself, taking his seat, and resting his handcuffed hands on his lap. Looking past the hardcore convict, Roman could see other convict's he knew being loaded onto the F.B.O.P plane. Leaning back into the thick cushion of the prison bus seat, Roman, closed his eyes and tried to get some rest, but he could get the bar-clad window's and transfer plane out of his head. Briefly opening his eyes, he shook his head and wished that he could awake from the bad dream he was having.

MMMM-VRRRR-OOOMMMM. the bus ignition started and idled. Suddenly two guards with shot guns boarded the bus; one watched as the other went to a cage in the back of the bus, and looked himself inside of it. Then the other guard locked: another cage that separated the convicts from the driver and himself and then he took his seat. For the entire ride, he gripped his shotgun and surveyed the convict's for any suspicious movements.

The bus was quiet with the exception of the loud hum of the diesel engine, and small chatter amongst the convicts aboard the transport vehicle named the Blue Bird. In-and-out of deep contemplation, Roman, thought of his son, of Diva and his mother. By the second, he got mad and very upset about subjecting himself to such treatment but dared not to complain openly about it. Twisting his wrist inside of his cuffs, he tried to get as comfortable as he could. He knew he had a long torturous expedition ahead of him. He was on his way to prison he knew nothing about. Roman's thoughts of him having to meet new people made him shake his head. He would have to figure out a new hustle, how to get drugs into the prison and find trustworthy convicts to move them behind prison walls. Until he could figure all of that out, he would keep to himself, and avoid being part of anyone's clique or gang. Through jailhouse conversation, he heard that in a real prison, blacks hung with blacks, Hispanics with Hispanics, whites with whites, and if you were from a certain state or a part of a gang, you hung with them. Roman heard that this was the only way to survive behind the wall. If you didn't want to be a part of a gang then you had to join a religious group. A lot of hustlers became Muslim for protection. It was all too much for Roman to figure out at that moment, so he closed his eyes, and fell asleep.

THREE HOURS LATER, Roman, was awakened by several conversations being held on the bus. Wiping his eyes with his cuffed hands, and tuned in to what was being said. As far as what he was picking up on no one on the bus had less than ten years, and they all were from at least a dozen different States: Baltimore, D.C, Cleveland, Detroit, and Pittsburgh to name a few.

Roman and the tattooed face convict next to him listened in silence. Neither one of them said a word. Despite the mean mug on the tatted convict's face, Roman knew that he was just as nervous as everyone else on the bus. The stories circulating throughout the close quarters of the transportation bus were about convicts that met their demise behind the walls. One individual came in with 48 months and caught a life sentence right before his release date. Roman wasn't trying to have that happen to him, but at the same time, he knew that he couldn't let any motherfucker punk him. As the tatted face convict lean back into his seat, Roman could tell that the trip was taking its toll on him. Taking a quick glimpse at the convict, Roman, recognized a Blood-affiliated tattoo on his face. Roman also had tattoos but none of them were gang-related, and Roman was happy of that fact. Because he

Our Love Is A Life Sentence

knew that being part of a gang behind the wall could mean that you would be forced to murder or be murdered.

"I'm tellin' you now if ya know if ya paperwork ain't right ya ass betta check in. Cause ma'fuckas ain't playin' dat rat shit behind dat ma'fuckin' gate," One convict reminded the other. Roman knew all about having to have his paperwork in order. He had Diva put his (P.5.1) Presentence Investigation Report and his Sentencing transcript's to the side. But he also heard that convicts could also check another convicts background out on the Law Library computer. Either way Roman was worried about it. He knew that he could prove that he was a stand-up nigga with ease.

"Where they got you goin' to?" The tatted face convict asked Roman, finally saying something.

"USP Canaan," Roman replied.

"Me too," the tatted face convict replied.

"Damn, it's ah few of us goin' up dat bitch. I had my people look dat joint up. She said dat they was locked. It was like two stabbings up dat bitch," another convict chimed in.

"Yeah, I just came from up there. It's ugly up dat bitch," another convict added.

"Fuck!!" Roman thought, leaning back into his seat. Now he had to prepare himself for being locked into a cell for twenty-four hours a day with a stranger that could turn out to be his enemy, depending on what State he was from.

AT DIVA'S HOUSE, she was woke up by the ringing of her phone. Jumping up from Dice's arms, she frantically looked for her cell phone. She thought it was Roman calling her, but it was his lawyer, "Yeah, she answered.

"I got some valuable information fo' you Diva. When can we meet," Sam Sholar asked.

"What kind of information," Diva asked, looking over at Dice. Dice sat up on the bed.

"They kind of information I need fifty thousand dollars for." "FIFTY THOUSAND DOLLARS?!"

"Look, I can't say no more about it over the phone. Meet me at our spot in a hour, and bring the money," Attorney Sam Sholar said before hanging up the phone.

"Who was that," Dice asked.

"Sam. He wants to meet in ah hour, and he wants me to bring fiddy stacks."

"Fiddy stacks fo' what?!"

"He said he has valuable information."

"It better be valuable. Cause if it ain't I'ma take dat fiddy stacks right back off his ass," Dice said, standing up to stretch.

"Thanks, fo' stayin' wit' me last night, bro," Diva said, walking over to Dice to hug him. Although they had slept in the same bed nothing happened between them. They had slept on top of the bed covers fully dressed.

"No problem, sis. Hey tho, I'm sittin' here thinkin' an' shit, you said you wanna get Roman out right..."

"Yeah. Fuck yeah, bro!"

'...And dude said he got some valuable info fo' you..."

"Mm hmm," Diva stepped back from Dice and cocked her head to the side. She was curious to know what his brain was conjuring up. "...Well, maybe we can use dat info to get bro out."

"You serious?! How?!"

"Come on, let's take a ride to the spy shop, downtown."

CHAPTER 19 BALANCE OF JUSTICE

DIVA WALKED INTO STARBUCKS and instantly spotted Sam Sholar. She took a seat across from him, and sat her new purse on the table, "What's goin' on Sam." Diva asked.

"First of all, how are you. I just got the news that you were kidnapped last night," said the Attorney, wearing a Steel Ballon Bleu watch, with seven-hundred-dollar Palladium Diablo de Cartier pen sticking out of the pocket of his Hilburn two-button wool jacket, that covered his cotton shirt by Gucci.

"I'm good. Thank God the police were there at the right time," Diva said, blowing out air with a deflated expression on her face, "It was a crazy night."

"Yes, it was. A few of my friends were injured at the explosion on Penn," Sam Sholar said, not knowing that Diva's childhood friends were the ones that caused the explosion, and killed the cop at the scene.

"Sorry to hear that, but what you got fo' me Sam? I'm in kind of a rush. I gotta go pick my son up from his grandmother's."

Our Love Is A Life Sentence

"I'm sorry. I didn't mean to hold you up. I just wanted to make sure you were okay, but umm, did you know the gentleman that tried to kidnap you?"

"No. He called me and said that he had money fo' Roman, and when
I, got there he pulled out a gun and forced me to get in his trunk."

"Wow! Well, the guys name is Ross Farrier, on the streets he's known as 'Smooth.' The government knows him as CS1."

11CS1?! 11

"Yes, he's a Confidential Source for the government."

"WHAT?! And he's out here kidnappin' bitches, an' shit!"

"Good thing he did try to kidnap you.

"What da fuck you mean lucky he tried to kidnap me" Diva snapped, winding her neck around, and screw facing the attorney.

"Listen, I didn't mean it like that. But it's because he tried to kidnap you that the government no longer haves a case. He was scheduled to testify in front of a Grand Jury next week. Now the government's only source of information is an unreliable source."

"So, they no longer have a case?"

"They no longer have a case? Hold up, what was this case about?"

"As far as I can see the guy Smooth made a deal with the government. He was supposed to get out, and set up one of Roman's friend. Smooth told the government that Roman's friend was going to set him up for business once he got out. They were going to set up a controlled buy, and link Roman to it," Sam Sholar said, sliding a leather zipper folder by Smythson over to Diva.

"That's crazy because Roman don't set nobody up. Plus, he doesn't have anyone out here that could do anything like that for him,"

Diva said, unzipping the folder to read the contents inside of it.

"Also, they were trying to tie a murder to Roman..."

"A MURDER, WHAT MURDER?!" Diva said, looking up from the documents.

"Ssshhh, keep it down, Diva. As far as I read one of Roman's friends was killed not too long ago. Smooth said that he wasn't sure if Roman was involved with it or not, but the government was also trying to tie the body to him. They were planning on giving Roman a life sentence behind all of this."

Our Love Is A Life Sentence

"Oh my god. Dis is crazy. Is dis my copy?" Diva asked, listening to Sam while she read the notes from Smooth's proffer session."

"Nooo, I can't give you that. That has to go back to where I got it from. I just wanted you to read so that you know that I wasn't lying to you about the information I had for you,' Did you bring the money?"

"Yeah, here you go," Diva said, going into her purse to pull out a large manila envelope. Digging inside of it she pulled out a ten-thousand-dollar stack and handed it to the attorney.

"Whoa Diva, just give me the envelope," Sam Sholar said, looking around for any suspicious spectators.

"Oh sorry, Sam. Here you go and thank you. I really appreciate it."

"No problem. If I hear anything else I'll give you a heads up." "Dat's what's up."

"Alright, let me get out of here. I need to return this folder and be in Court. Hey, tell Roman I send my regards."

"Will do, Sam. Take care," Diva said, watching as the attorney departed.

Our Love Is A Life Sentence

INSIDE OF DICE'S SUV, "What was he talkin' bout, sis," Roman asked Diva.

"He had a folder with all this shit in it about Roman, about you, and about dat nigga dat kidnapped me."

"About Roman ... About me. Where the folder at. I need to see dat, A.S.A.P!"

"He took it back, but hopefully we got everything he told me on videotape."

"Here you go, bro," Diva handed Dice the purse they had purchased from the Spyware store. It was equipped with a miniature camcorder.

"Grab my laptop from the backseat, sis," Dice said, taking the SD card from out of the miniature camcorder inside of the purse.

He gave Diva the purse back, and took the laptop, "Now let's see what we got," Dice said, powering up his laptop, and inserting the SD card into a slot. After a couple seconds the footage popped up on the screen.

"Dat shit's clear as fuck, Diva said.

"Hell yeah," Dice said, pushing play.

'What's goin' on Sam...'

'First of all, how are you. I just got the news that you were kidnapped last night ...''

Our Love Is A Life Sentence

'I'm good. Thank God, the police were there at the right time. It was a crazy night ...'

'Yes, it was...'

"Bro, fast forward ah lil bit," Diva told Dice.

Watching the footage, *'Well, the guys name is Ross Farrier, on the streets he's known as 'Smooth.' The government knows him as CS1 ...'*

"He's talkin' bout dat piece of shit dat kidnapped me," Diva added.

"Yes, he's a Confidential Source for the government...WHAT?! And he's out here kidnappin' bitches, an' shit," Dice pressed fast forward again.

'It's because he tried to kidnap you that the government no longer haves a case. He was scheduled to testify in front of a Grand Jury next week. Now the government's only source of information is an unreliable source... So, they no longer have a case ...'

'What was the case about?'

The guy Smooth made a deal with the government.

"Who's Smooth?" Dice asked.

"Dat's dude that kidnapped me."

"Oh, okay. Dat's his street name. He did to get out and set one of Roman's friend government that Roman's friend was going once he got out ... Did Roman say anything didn't say shit to me."

bro. You know I never even heard say Dat ... He was supposed. Smooth told them to set him up for business bout dat. He definitely of dude.'

Me neither these ma'fuckas was just try'na build some shit. Shit's crazy, "Dice said.

Watching Attorney Sam Sholar past Diva the leather zipper folder, *"Also they were trying to tie a murder to Roman ...*

"A MURDER, WHAT MURDER?! What murder is he talkin' bout, sis?" Dice asked, fully at attention now.

"I think he was talkin' bout Ewee, bro."

"How the fuck they tie dat shit to bro? I never talked to him bout dat, did you?!" Dice asked, pressing pause on the laptop.

"Hell no. I know they be recording dem conversations on dem phone's, an' shit. He had seen dat shit on the news, but the only thing we talked about concerning dat was the wake. I told him we was goin' to the wake, but dat's it!"

"Shit's crazy cause I know they ain't got shit far as dat, but we gotta be super careful. These ma'fuckas is prolly all over us," Dice said, pressing play on the laptop.

"Smooth said that he wasn't sure if Roman was involved with it or not, but the government was also trying to tie the

Our Love Is A Life Sentence

body to him. They were planning on giving Roman a life sentence behind all of this. Sis, dis shit is mad!"

"It's crazy to say, but Sam was right. It's a good thing dat dis lame tried to kidnap me cause the only reason these ma'fuckas don't have a case no mo'."

"Right?!" Dice said, watching the footage.

'Did you bring the money?' 'Yea, here you go---'

"GOT EEEEMMM!" Dice said as he watched the attorney accept the money provided to him by Diva.

"Bro, you still didn't tell me how dis is goin' to get Roman out?"

Hm hm hm hm.

Dice chuckled, "Sis, dem ma'fuckas tried to come at us, but we bout to go at these ma'fuckas haaarrrd, you hear me?! First, I'ma find out if they still on us," Dice said, looking out of his SUV at their surroundings, "Then we gon' take dis footage to my lawyer, and have him make a deal with the same ma'fuckas dat's try'na book my bro fo' life."

"What kind of deal, bro?"

'Sis, dem ma'fuckas would do anything to keep dis shit on the hush, includin' lettin' bro out on Immediate Release."

"What's Immediate Release?"

"It's when the Judge makes the government let ah nigga go, immediately!"

"Awww, bro, fo' real. I fuckin' love you. Ya smart as shit fo' dis," Diva said, hugging Dice, "So once we give the lawyer dis Roman ah be home?"

"Well, da process ah prolly take ah week or two, but it shouldn't take no longer."

"AH WEEK OR TWO. OH, MY GOD, THANK YOU, JESUS! THANK YOU SOOO MUCH, BRO!" Diva said, excited by the news.

"But first, let me check some shit out. I'ma hold on to dis, and we'll go see the lawyer later today or first thing in the mornin'."

"Kay," Diva was completely humbled by the news.

"Try'na give my man's life fo' some bullshit. Try'na fuck wit' us. Try'na fuck wit' me. Naaah, naw, I ain't goin' out like dat ... We ain't goin' out like dat!" Dice said, closing the laptop, and staring into abyss.

CHAPTER 20 THE ONE THAT GOT AWAY

AT THE DISTRICT ATTORNEY'S OFFICE, District Attorney Mary Goldberg met with agents Martin Dunbar and Arthur Galloway, "So because of this idiot Farrier we no longer have a case against Edmonds," the DA asked.

"I'm afraid not," agent Dunbar replied.

"What about the guy he was supposed to meet when he got out," the DA asked.

"Unfortunately, we never found out who that was," agent Dunbar replied.

"Well, what about the murder, anything?!"

"Hmmm, no. Nothing. This guy really fouled up for us."

"I thought this guy was supposed to be on home monitor?"

"He was, but it takes a few days for that all to be set up."

"Mm mm mm, I cannot fuckin' believe this. Just days ago, we had this guy looking at a life sentence, now we got nothing. But I tell you who is going to pay, this guy Farrier. I'm really going to cook his ass, and I hope he tries to go to trial."

"I could kill this guy," agent Galloway added.

"Where is this guy at now," the DA asked.

"Currently at the Allegheny County Jail," agent Galloway answered. "I want you guys to go see this son of a bitch. Maybe he'll hear something while his ass sits and rots," the DA said.

"We're all over him," agent Galloway replied before the two agents left out of the DA's office.

Our Love Is A Life Sentence

AT THE LAW OFFICE OF Gibson & Sumpter, Dice and Diva met with Attorney at Law Melissa Suripter, "This is unbelievable," the attorney said to her new client after reviewing the footage they gave her.

"Do you think it will get my husband immediately released?" Diva asked.

"Ha, that's the least that this will do," Mrs. Edmonds," attorney Sumpter said.

"So, what's our next move?" Dice asked.

"Our next move is me going, meet with the District Attorney to make a deal with her."

"But you'll make it though, right?!" Dice questioned.

"Yes. Of course, for Mr. Edmonds release in a week or two," the attorney said before releasing the footage to her, "Then I'll file a petition with the Court's and more and likely, he'll be home in a week or two."

AT ALLEGHENY COUNTY JAIL
VISITATION, Ella was visiting Grinch, "You alright?" Grinch asked Ella.

"Yeah. I'm still ah lil shook up, but I'm good," Ella said, staring at Grinch through the scratched plexiglass that separated the two of them.

"Are you goin' to go to ya mom's or what?"

"Grinch, I'm not goin' nowhere, you hear me!"

"El', don't be stupid. Ma'fuckas might come back at you, an' shit. You need to go on an' get up outta there, at least fo' a minute. You got fifty stacks. Them ma'fuckas ain't give you dat paper fo' nothin'. They want you out the way, and they try'na make sure I don't say shit," Grinch said into the phone, looking Ella in her eyes.

"Are you goin' to say anything?"

"Fuck no! Fuck these ma'fuckas. Ma'fuckas had me held up questioning me all last night. They ain't got shit but my new charges, and I'll prolly do like forty-eight months, fo' dat shit."

"Forty-eight months?!"

"Yeah, dat ain't really shit, tho, El'. Now dat you got dat money we straight. For now, tho you just need to lay low. Let dis shit calm down."

"What about that Bigga Figga an' Timbo shit, bae?"

"El', fuck dem niggas. They shot up the spot. They could have killed you. Killed the kids. I ain't thinkin' bout dem niggas. The Feds tried to ask me about dem niggas. They was like, "Why they shoot ya baby mama's house up," I was like, "I don't know."

"Why did they shoot my house up?"

"El, I'm not gettin' into dat wit' you. You good now. They dead, you got dat paper, and we straight. I ain't no rat. I don't care if Dice didn't send me dat money. I don't have shit to say to the Feds."

"Oh, dat's who sent the money, Dice? Is he the one dat killed Ewee?"

"Yea, he sent dat money, but I don't know who killed cuz. Even if I did I wouldn't tell you. Dat's street shit, and it's gon stay in the streets. I'm already mad I got you an' the kids dis involved in dis shit ... Fuck, it's time to wrap it up," Grinch said, seeing the lights blinking off and on. That was a signal that told the visitor's that they had five minutes left of their visiting hour.

"Love you I'll be back tomorrow," Ella said, kissing her hand and placing it
to the plexiglass. "Love you too. Bring the kids tomorrow," Grinch said, doing the same.

LEAVING OUT OF THE US ATTORNEY'S OFFICE, Attorney Sumpter placed a call to Dice, he was at Diva's house. They were smoking and talking about everything that was going on. Early that day, Dice had sent Blonde two hours out of town to a truck stop. He wanted to see if anyone followed her on the Pennsylvania Turnpike. Through counter surveillance, he found out that she was good to make another move. He knew that the Feds were grasping at straws, but he wanted to make sure that they weren't hot. "Hol' up, dis the lawyer," Dice said
to the female gangsters, "Yeah, what's goin' on," he said as he answered his cell phone.
"Hello, Dice. I got great news. Your Mr. Edmonds will be home real soon..."
"FUCK YEA! HELL YEA, DAT'S WHAT'S UP!!"
"...I just left a meeting with the US Attorney and District Attorney Goldberg. They accepted the deal a few seconds after seeing the footage. I gave them a copy of the footage, and I also gave them a copy of the serial numbers that you guys gave me. I told them to check the fifty dollar bills. Annnd I'm starting the paperwork for your friend's release. The judge will have it in the morning, and your friend should be released in 7-to-10 days at the most."

"Thank you! I really appreciate you. Dis is good lookin' out.

I can't wait to talk to my man to let him know he'll be home soon..."

"WHEN?! WHEN, BRO?! WHEN IS HE GETTIN' OUT," Diva asked, jumping up and down.

"...7-to-10 days, sis. Calm ya lil ass down," Dice said, watching Diva jump for joy while Blonde and Evette looked on with smiles on their faces. They had never met Roman, but had heard all about him, and knew that he was the man behind their street god.

"Once the paperwork goes through I will call you and the jail Mr. Edmonds, to inform them about his release. What jail is he currently at? the attorney asked.

"He's up Youngstown Ohio."

"Okay. well, it's just a waiting game now."

"Might thanks," Dice said before hanging up with his attorney. Proud of the move he made, it was a dirty one, but effective. He had checkmated the United States government.

CHAPTER 21 BAWSS MEETS BAWSS

Several hours after leaving Youngstown Ohio Roman finally met his destination and he was grateful that the road trip had come to an end. He wished that he could have slept the entire way there but the last couple of hours of the transfer had him up and wide-eyed. He was sick of hearing the war-stories and jailhouse tales. All he wanted to do was get to a cell so that he could get settled in and face whatever hellish fate that awaited him. But before all of that, he knew that he would have to spend several hours in R&D. He would have to be processed into the new jail. As the transportation bus pulled up a huge steel gateway automatically opened. The Federal Penitentiary was massive and surrounded by two electric razor barb wire fences and gun towers. The prison was intimidating, but Roman kept his composure. He tried to manage his nervousness but it was hard to quell his anxiety. When he heard the giant steel gate closed behind them he realized that he had arrived at the F.B.O. P's destination for him. Once the bus halted the guard's moved to ready themselves. First, the guard sitting up front freed the shotgun toting guard from his cage in the back of the bus and escorted him to the outside of the bus, shotgun in hand. Then the convicts were shuffled off the bus and walked into the propylaeum of the U.S.P, and lined up against the two-mile long corridor. Then they were freed of their shackles and cuffs and asked the name and prison, number by a guard that worked at the institution. When three of the convict's names were called they were asked to step out of line, Roman included.

"What, the fuck is going on," Roman asked himself.

"You three come with me," another guard said before leading the trio down the hallway into R&D, "Step into this cell," the guard told them.

"Yo, what the fuck is this?!" Roman asked one of the other convicts.

"I think this is because we're going to the camp," the skinny white convict with long-stringy blonde hair.

"The Camp, you think that's where we going? My man told' me that's where I was goin' but my counselor never confirmed dat shit," Roman said.

"What's ya level?" The white convict asked.

"I'ma level one," Roman replied.

"Yeah, you goin' to the Camp too."

"Damn, that's what's up," Roman said., feeling a sense of relief.

"Edmonds, come on," a guard said, opening the cell door. Roman followed the guard to a dressing room with two large containers of jailhouse clothes and shoes in them.

"What's ya sizes," the guard asked.

"Three-X shirt ... 40 in pants and 10 in shoes."

"Might, here you go. Strip down and put these on. What you want to do wit' ya clothes, destroy them or donate them." the guard asked.

"Donate 'em."

"Reynolds," the guard called out, and as Roman was going back into the holding cell the long stringy-haired white boy walked out.

"Man, dis is crazy. I know dis ain't what they gon' have us rocking' in dis bitch," Roman said looking over the Khaki outfit and blue-and-white skipper shoes he had on.

"Ha ha ha, prolly not. We prolly get some more clothes when we get down to the Camp," the third convict said. He was about 5'6, dark skin and muscular.

"Why da fuck they separate us from the rest of dem ma'fuckas," Roman asked, hoping the convict could give him some insight.

"Campers aren't allowed to be around inmates that's goin' to the Pen. Them ma'fuckas would have tried to fuck us up if they knew that we were going to the Camp.

"Damn, dat's crazy," Roman said.

"Phelps," the guard called for the last convict in the holding cell.

Then one-by-one the three inmates were fingerprinted and photographed for personal jailhouse identifications. Afterward they were lead into a conference room where they were interviewed and made aware of the prison policies. "In case of an emergency or death who would you like us to contact or send your body," the guard asked after having Roman sign a few documents.

"Diva, Devanna British. Her number is 2-7-7-0-5-2-1," Roman replied. Then he was given a red-and-white ID card and lead back to the holding cell. Once all three inmates were interviewed they were lead past two larger holding cells that held the other inmates that were transported with them. Roman couldn't help but to feel a sort of sympathy for the convicts that would have to

be subjected to the harsh conditions of the maximum part of the Federal prison.

Lead back in to, the hallway they were uncuffed the three inmates waited for a few moments before they were escorted to the giant steel entrance they were driven in to but this time they were uncuffed and told to exit out of a door that was on the right side of the impervious entranceway, "Just stand here. Your ride should be here shortly," is all the guard said before stepping back into the doorway and locking the door behind her.

"What the fuck... Is dis ah set-up ... Dis gots to be a fuckin' setup... Our ride," Roman tossed a few thoughts around in his head as all three of the inmates looked around, studying razor-layered fenced facility.

"Yo Get in. Come on. I ain't got all day," someone pulled up in a white 2015 white Ford Explorer and said. Roman and the other two inmates looked at each other, puzzled by what was going on. "Man, these ma'fuckin' Feds don't give up. They still try'na trick me in to cooperating," Roman said, the last to enter the SUV.

"Y'all smoke?" The white Fed-looking driver asked.

"Naw," Roman replied.

"Yea ... Me too," The other inmates answered. 'Wight. I'ma take y'all down here. Get y'alls clothes and linened and then we'll go out to smoker's row. We ain't 'lowed to smoke. Hell, we ain't 'lowed to drink, but we do that shit anyway. You know how it is, they make the rules and we find ways to break the rules," the driver said, slumped down in the driver seat like a homie from the hood.

"Hol' up, you ah inmate," Roman dumbfoundedly asked.

"Ha ha...Yea, I'ma an inmate ... Ha: ha," the driver answered as they pulled in to a gateless parking lot, "I'ma check y'all in wit'

the C.O. and I'll get y'all situated and take y'all to y'alls Unit," the driver said, "By the way I'm Greek. If y'all ever need anything, just give me ah holla," Greek said, exiting the SUV and shaking their hands.

"I'm Lynch," the white stringy haired blonde said, "Do you know Canon," he asked Greek.

"Yea, I know 'im. I'll bake you to 'im after I dress y'all out. Where you from?"

"West Virginia."

"And y'all," Greek asked.

"Baz, I'm from Philly," said the dark skin muscular inmate said.

"We got some Philly duds here ... And you," Greek said to Roman, extending his hand.

"Roman, I'm from the West of Pitt...Pittsburgh."

Our Love Is A Life Sentence

"Oh yeah. I'm from Wes Mifflin ... We got homies here. .You know Young Bucky?"

"Yeah, I know Bucky," Roman said, shaking Greek's hand.

"Y'all gon' love it here, it's wide open here," Greek said, leading them into the Officer's message-center.

After dressing the three inmates out, Greek, lead them to the Unit and their assigned bunk area. It was an open dorm, "YOOOOO, Roman, what up, fam'?!" A short wavy-haired, stalky inmate in a gray sweat suit and Tim's announced with his hands extended out to Roman.

"Buck! What up, baby. I ain't seen ya ass in ah minute," Roman said, embracing his Pittsburgh homie. Buck was from Braddock PA but the two of them knew each other from their getting-money days. The frequented the same clubs and heard of and respected each other. Roman knew of Bucky's case and knew he was stand up.

"Boy, I ain't seen you in ah minute."

"Rome man, I been down goin' on seven. I'm out next year." "Damn, it been dat long?!"

"Fuck yea"

"Shit, I see ya ass got all swole up, an' shit! Ha ha ha..." you know. Nigga try'na go home lookin' good, you know?!' What size shoe you wear," Bucky asked.

"10-10. 1/2."

291

"Got you. I got some Butter's fo' you and some Jay's. Plus, me an' the homies gon' put ah nice care-package togetha fo' you..." "ROOO-MAAAN!! What up, baby?!"
"B-J, what up, yo. Damn fam', it's been a while." Roman and BJ grew up together. Although they were from different hoods they went to middle school together. Roman was from the West and BJ was from the Northside of Pittsburgh.
"Yo, I'ma go grab you some shit. Me and my man Dee-Lew. Yeah,

dig my man Derek Lewis. He from the Rocks, you know him," BJ asked. "Nah, but I think I heard of you, tho'."
"Yeah, we most definitely know some of the same peoples," Dee-Lew said, not minding that BJ gave Roman his government name. It was a coded way to tell other inmates that who they were rolling with were stand-up men.
"Aight, come on, fam'. Put dat shit in ya locker. I'ma take you to get you some sweat suits, boots, shoes ... You smoke?" "Nah, I don't smoke cigarettes."
"I ain't just talkin' bout cigarette's ... Do you smoke, nigga?!" "Hell yea, then. I smoke!"
'Wight, we gon' blaze, we gon drink, I got some Henny. I'ma get you ah lil celly, so you can talk to ya people..."

"Celly?!"

"Yea fam', I gotta iPhone 6 fo you to rock out wit'...So you can talk to ya people off the radar, an' shit, you know."

"Damn, dat's what's up. I ain't talk to my people since yesterday."

"Well, 1 got you. Dam' dat ten ain't gon' be nothin' here. I GOT YOU!" Bucky said. Hearing him mentioned his ten-year sentence let Roman know that Bucky and possibly the others knew about his case.

"Yo, I'ma have my people screen-shot my paperwork so you an' the rest of the homies will know I'm straight."

"Fam, I already know you straight. You ain't gotta worry bout dat. The streets already solidified ya thoroughness. You good here, I'm vouching' fo' you."

"My man," Roman said, embracing Bucky, feeling good about his new living arrangements. Not knowing that he wouldn't be there for too long.

CHAPTER 22 CAMP LIFE

Roman had heard stories about being in a Federal Camp, but being there was nothing like he imagined. It was wide open. There were no walls, fences or barbwire. The inmates drove or walked a block or two to work each morning. It was nothing like being in jail at all.

After getting Roman situated, Bucky, showed Roman around and introduced him to the stand-up men in the Camp and told him who to stay away from.

"Come on, big dawg. Let's hit the track," Bucky told Roman. "Here you go," he said, handing Roman an iPhone 6 with the headphone set.

"Damn, dis shit's crazy ... Ha ha," Roman said as he stuffed the phone into the pouch of his hoodie, looking around as he did so.

"Yeah, dat shit's already set up. All you gotta do is turn it on. Give ya people dis number and tell her to call my people A.S.A.P. I'ma get you a visit prolly tomorrow. I know you wanna holla at ya people ... "

"DO I?! Dat visit behind the glass is fo' suckas."

Our Love Is A Life Sentence

"It normally takes about ah week fo' the counselor to get'cha visiting list approved but I got a way around dat. But in the morning I'ma take you to see the counselor to get'cha pin-numbers so you can use the computers and phones. And when you talk to ya girl tell her to give you her email so that y'all could set up ah TRU-Links account."
"Dat's fo' us to email each other?"
"Yea-yup ... And I'ma get you ah job up there with me and BJ. It's ah night job but it's cool. I'm in good with the C.O. up there she's good people. When I go up there tonight I'ma tell her wassup, and tomorrow you'll leave with us around Eleven tomorrow night."
"Dat's wassup. I'm wit' dat."
'Wight let go over to the bleachers," Bucky said, leading Roman over to a group of inmates, some he had been introduced to, and others he nodded to. Roman could smell Loud in the air, and seen a bottle of Henny being passed around. Bucky got red plastic
drinking cup, handed it to Roman, and pour him ah drink. Roman couldn't believe how open the Camp was. "Good Lookin'," he said, taking sips of the Henny.
"No problem, big dawg. I tol' you I got you," Bucky said as he pulled out his cell-phone and starting using it.

295

"It's cool," Roman asked as he gestured by tapping the pouch of his hoodie.

"Yeah, go head, big dawg. Eh'body good people here," Bucky said. As he said it BJ locked eyes with Roman, smiled and nodded his head upwards. He and a few others were already using their cell-phones.

"Set ya screen-lock up before you do anything, big dawg," Bucky told Roman.

"Might got you," after setting up his screen-lock and password, Roman finally called Diva. It took him three attempts before she answered, "WHO'S DIM!" She yelled into the phone, frustrated that she had not spoken to Roman. Roman's homie had called her

from Youngstown and told her that he had been transferred, but the number Roman was calling from had a 4-1-2 Area Code.

"It's me, baby," Roman said, calmly.

"HUSSSS-BAAAANNND!! Baby, where you at, husband?!"

"The Camp up Canaan."

"Where's Canaan?"

"Waymart PA."

"I'll be there within' the next couple days."

"Oh look, my man what you to hook up wit' his girl and come up wit her. I'll text you her info when we hang up."
"Hold on, husband. Ya number says 4-1-2 and there wasn't no annoying ass recording. How the hell is you on ah cell phone ... ha ha."
"I'm on my Master P shit, I got da hook up ... Ha ha ha."
"Don't get in no trouble guess what, bae," Diva said, somberly. "What, what's wrong?!"
"I got kidnapped last night."
"WHAT?!! What you mean?!"
"Ya old celly tricked me. He said he had some money fo' me, and when I met him, he forced me in the trunk."
"GET DA FUCK OUTTA HERE! YOU BULLSHITTIN'!"
"Look, I popped the trunk from the inside and a police officer was right in back of us," hearing what happened made Roman furious. He was so hot that he couldn't say anything. Tears filled the rims of his eyes, "Tomorrow when you come up here I'm leaving' wit' you. I'ma kill dat nigga!"
"No, bae. They got him. They locked him up, and guess what..." "Hmph, what?!"
"Because he did dat shit you coming home."
"What... What you mean?

"... The Fed's was try'na build ah case against you. He told them all dis bullshit about. Try'na say you had some'in' to do wit'
Ewee's murda..."
"What?! I 'don't know shit bout dudes murda."
"Look, me and bro got you ah new lawyer and eh' thang. She put a motion in, and you gon' be coming home real soon..."
"COUNT TIME. COUNT TIME," a guard announced over the outside PA-system cutting their conversation short.
"Wifey, I gotta go. They just called count. I'ma hit you later." "Love you I'ma text you bro's number, call him he'll tell you more about what's goin' on"
"A'ight, love you."
"Love you, too
"We allowed back out here after count?" Roman asked Bucky as they walked back to the housing unit.
"Yeah, we can be out here 'til twelve
"Fam, don't you know my old celly got out and kidnapped my wifey!"
"Straight up?! She a'ight?'"
'Yea, she's cool. She said because of that I'm supposed to be gettin' released or some shit You ever hear of anything like dat?"

"Nah, dat's crazy. Unless she gon' testify on her kidnapper to get you out I don't know."

"Shit, me neither. I'ma hit my man's after count and find out what exactly is goin' on."

CHAPTER 23 GETTIN' DUG IN

AFTER NINE O'CLOCK COUNT, Roman, made a couple calls. First, he called Dice, "Yo bro, what's goin' on out there?"

"What up,' big bro?! Dis how you do it celly an' shit? Ha ha," Diva told Dice that Roman would be calling him but he didn't know that he would be calling him on a cell phone.

"You know how we do, homie."

"Bro, so much shit been happenin'. It's cool to talk on dis joint, ain't it. My shit's fresh out the box," Dice asked, referring to their phones.

"Yea-yup."

"You heard about Bigga Figga, right?"

"Nah, I was in transit. I heard about Ewee tho."

"Dat's the body the Fed's was try'na put on you."

"What?! I ain't have shit to do wit' dat nigga gettin' killed. I ain't even fuck wit dat nigga, fo' real," Roman said with his face etched in confusion and frustration.

"Well dat nigga Bigga Fig now, too."

"What you mean? What da fuck, what happened?"

"Dem two crazy ma'fuckas de they did a drive-by on da bo garand one of his soldier's is dead, declared war on the 5-0. After Grinch's BM's spot."

"Shit's goin' down out dat bitch. News, an' all dat!!"

"Psss, dat shit's crazy. "Man bro, dat shit was on CNN!"

"Get da fuck outta here?!"

"Straight up. But like .1 said, dat nigga Ewee's body is the one the Fed's tried to tie to you, but they ain't got shit. It's all 'bout some shit ya celly tol' dem"

"But I ain't tell dat lame shit 'bout nobody," Roman said, thinking back, "Oh shit!"

"What?!"

"Naw, Diva came to see me and told me 'bout the boy gettin' murked, an' me an' him had ah convo 'bout dat shit, but I don't know nothin' 'bout dat shit. I don't know who did dat shit, an' I sure ain't tell him nothin'!"

"We did dat shit, big bro. My big ultimatum. His man Grinch pistol-whipped her in da hospital. Split her shit hide dat nigga. So, my other chick."

"Hol'! Dat's enough, fam'. We'll to-face. But ah, know you can't hit dat nigga. I gave dat p one of my girl's, an' put ide-open. An' he was try'na to have to talk 'bout dat face-leave no loose ends."

"Nah, my bitches are straight. They stand up broads."

"I'm just sayin' you never know I don't want you facin' ah life sentence."

"Nah big bro, our love fo' each other is ah life sentence. We all bonded fo' life. Ain't none of us crossin' each other."

"I feel you. like I said we'll talk face-to-face 'bout it. But yo, keep dat shit on da hush, an' tell dem bitches to keep they mouths shut."

"Oh, they know. They some thorough bitches. An' far as face-to-face, nigga ... I'ma see you when they free you in ah matter of days. I know Diva tol' you. We gettin' you outta dat bitch!"

"Yeah, she was tellin' me some shit, but she ain't tell me how y'all was gettin' me out, an'shit."

"Yo, da nigga dat 'napped Diva was slippin'. He put sis' in da trunk, an' I put Deev' on game on how to pop dat bitch from the inside. An' sis' popped da trunk, an' da ma'fuckin' 5-0 was

right behind her, an shit. So dat's how they booked him, but earlier today she gets ah call from ya lawyer. He want fiddy-stacks fo' some info he got."

"FIDDY-STACKS!! MAN, DAT FOOL'S TRIPPIN'!!"

"Dat's what I said, so we set dat fool up. Got 'im on tape trading' government information fo' dollars,"

Our Love Is A Life Sentence

"It's too much-shit goin on out dat bitch; murdas, kidnappin's, shoot-out's wit' da po-po. Shit, I'm scared to come home.. .Ha ha ha."

"Shit big bro, you comin' da fuck home. I need a fuckin' vacation ... But anyway, I took dat shit to my lawyer, an' she's makin' a deal fo' ya release. Oh an', as far as dat rat ass nigga, you ain't gotta worry 'bout him or d shit he tol' da feds bein' he tried to 'nap sis, ain't shit he said admissible in court!"

"Damn boy, you workin'!!"

"You know I'm doin' what I do fo' you. You looked out fo' me, an' I'm just returnin' da favor!"

"Like Jay said, 'Real Niggas Do Real Thangs!"

"Hell yea!!"

"Well, I'ma make dis call. Send word up to Ohio 'bout what dat fuck-boy did to Diva."

'Wight. Lay low, tho, bro. Ya ass ah be out in ah matter of days, an' my ass ah be up there to get you, too."

"I'm lookin' forward to it. Love you, fam."

"Love you too, big bro."

Our Love Is A Life Sentence

HANGING UP WITH DICE, Roman, placed another call. This one to his mule Jarvis's girl, and gave her a message to give to Jarvis on their next visit, and told her to tell him about his possibility of release. Jarvis was looking at twenty- years, but if he played his hand right he would be home a lot sooner.

"I'll go up there tomorrow to give him ya message. Thanks, bro," Shauntae, Jarvis' girl said.

Hanging up with her, Roman, logged in to his Facebook page, and searched for Ewee and then Bigga Figga's. They were both flooded with condolence posts. Most of the people that left messages Roman knew.

EWEE'S FACEBOOK PAGE:

FIRST POST: When I close my eyes, I see your face. I miss you so much. I wish you were here so we could smoke and joke like we use to R.I.P EWEE...Ve

SECOND POST: I'm still fucked up that you're gone, and now Bigga and the lil homie Timbo, too. I guess you ain't wanna smoke alone lol...Love you too bro ... Man Man

Roman looked up at his surroundings. Bucky was talking on his cell as were a few other convicts, some were smoking and others were drinking. It was like he was back on the block the night had fell upon them. Where they sat

304

they could barely be seen. Roman was still shocked by how open the camp was. Shaking his head, he looked down at another one of the post on Ewee's Facebook page:

THIRD POST: RWG Ewee ... Bigga Figga and Timbo!!

The message was from Roman's sister, Syria. Clicking on her post, Roman, left a message in her inbox:

ROMAN'S MESSAGE TO SYRIA: "Sis, what's ya number?" SYRIA: "Who's this?!! How you get on my brother's page?!!" ROMAN: "Lol ... It's me, sis. What's ya number?"

SYRIA: "412-333-4444"

Roman pressed on the phone number and auto-dialed his sister's number. After two rings, Syria, answered: "Who's dis?!!'1

"I toll you it's me, sis!"

"BROTHER! I miss you!"

"Miss you too, sis!" "You comin' home, huh?"

"Dat's what they say."

"When? Diva toll me and ma you were comin' home, but she said she wasn't sure when tho."

"I 'on't know. They say in like ah week or two."

"Hmph, I can't wait." "Shit, you. Where's ma?"

"You know she's knocked out. You want me to wake her up?"

305

"Nah, I hit her to..."

"...Bro, I'm headed in. I'ma take ah shower and eat before I go to work," Bucky said, cutting into Roman's conversation with his sister. "Sis, I'ma hit you back later."

"Aw bro, you gotta go?!"

"Yeah. I'll hit you back later tho. Love you."

"Okay. Love you too."

Roman hung up his phone, tucked it and headed back into the unit with Bucky, "Bro, I appreciate all the lookin' out," he said to Bucky on the way in.

"Bro, you ain't seen nothin' yet. Wait 'til ya girl come up. You, gave her my girl's number, didn't you?"

"Yeah. I tol' her to call her soon as she hung up with me."

"A'ight. I'ma holla at my bitch when I get to work. And I'ma get you up there wit' me. My man dat was up there wit' me went home a couple days ago. I tol' dis dude I was goin' to get him up there, but fuck him. I'ma get you, up there instead."

AROUND 11:00 pm, Bucky, was called into work. He told BJ to look after Roman while he was at work. He also reminded Roman of the 12:00 am, 3:00 am and 5:00 am count's, "Make sure ya in ya bunk area when they come around to count you. My homies are gon' make sure you good while I'm gone," he told Roman.

Our Love Is A Life Sentence

THAT NIGHT, Roman, video-chatted with Diva. He even went into a bathroom stall and had video-sex with her. Whispering dirty verbals to her until they both ejaculated. Roman and Diva were in their glory. He didn't have to but if he did, Roman, wouldn't have minded doing his time there.

SIX O'CLOCK THE NEXT MORNING, Roman, was awakened by Bucky shaking his leg, "Get up, Fam. they about to call chow," Bucky told Roman, "Hand me ya jack, I'ma charge it up fo' you," he added.

After they ate breakfast, Bucky, went to sleep while Roman was on phone-charging duty. A couple hours later, Bucky, woke up and collected their phones, "I'ma put these up fo' ah few, and take you to see the counselor. Sit here, I'll be right back.

Our Love Is A Life Sentence

AT NINE O'CLOCK A.M., Bucky and Roman entered "Counselor Truman's office, "What's going on Bucky?" The Counselor asked.

"Dis is my man, I know him from the street's. I wanna get him up at the job wit' me. Ms. Flint said to tell you dat it was good wit' her."

"Aight. Let me add him to the payroll up there," he said, typing some info into the computer, "What's ya last name?"

"Edmonds"

"You just got here, right?"

"Yeah, yup, last night."

"Aight, here you go. You'll start tonight. Anything else?"

"Yeah, he need his log in and phone info."

"Aight—

Tap-tap .Tap-tap. . .Tap-tap-tap-tap. . .ZINNNNNN.

Here You go," the counselor tapped his fingers against the keyboard, and printed out Roman's info, and handed it to him, "I'll be call you for Orientation in a couple days, so listen for your name," he told Roman.

"Okay. Might. Urn, what about My visiting-list. Do I hav'tah fill another one out?" Roman asked the counselor, turning back towards him on the way out of the door.

"No. Don't worry about it. Lieutenant approve your last list, but if you want to add more people fill out another list."

"I gotta extra visiting list fo' you," Bucky said.

"Cool," Roman said as him and Lucky exited the counselor's office.

"Might put ya jail number in the top box, dat nine-digit number in the second box, scan ya fingerprint, and press agree," Bucky instructed Roman. They were in the Computer Room, and Bucky was teaching Roman how to gain access to his email and other accounts, "You check ya money here," Bucky said.

"CLICK!" Roman went to Account transactions and clicked on the enter button.

'Aight, you got money on ya account. So, you'll be able to go to the store tomorrow. I'll show you how to fill out the commissary slip later," Bucky said once he seen that Roman had $7500.00 in his account. 'Wight, click here to access ya email's. You won't have any email's until you add email addresses to ya contact-list, and you gotta fill out ya mailing list, and phone-list. It'll take like ah hour or two to get ya contacts approved. So, fill dat out, add all ya contact's and email's, and meet me back on the Unit," Bucky told Roman.

CHAPTER 24 IMMEDIATE RELEASE

TWO HOURS LATER, Roman, had went back to the computer room to print out mailing-labels and to check his email's. After entering his password's and scanning his thumb, he clicked on emails. There was one sent from Diva:

"My Rock, my warrior, my husband," the email started off. Putting a smile on Roman's face. And it continued:

Thoughts of you are never at far reach from me, and once you are released I promise that you will never again be this far from me as long as we live.

Husband, you give me comfort even the silence of your unspoken word makes me want to share all I am and everything I have to give with you. I long to be back in your loving arms. Where I know that I will be protected no matter what else happens.

God has given us the strength to carry on, and through his will to carry on. You have given me the courage to share the love that have brought us together and that will keep us united for the rest of our lives. With you back home where you belong, we can create more wonderful life lasting memories as a family. And finally, we can make it "official," and our love and vows will be the glue that will bond us together through sickness or health until death do us part!

Until we see each other keep me in your every thought, in your every dream, and pray for me.

Love your wife,

"Diva Edmonds"

"Hmph! We're gon' make it official," Roman whispered under his breath. Clicking on "Reply," he tapped his two fingers against the computer's keyboard, and responded:

My Queen, my everything, my wife,

What I feel for you has no space or time. It threads us together with strains of eternity and endless love. When I lay down at night and dream-I'm with you without limits. When I awake my thoughts of you have no restraints or limits.

My love for you is as deep as the abyss, but this depth of darkness that we are currently engulfed in will succumb to the light of your rays of beauty and thoughtfulness, hope and ambition.

The thought of your loyalty and devotion strengthens me and makes me stand up tall. It humbles me and brings me to joyous tears. I thank God for the gift of you that he has given me.

You are my energy and the brightness of my life. You are the perfect cure when I'm sick. or down and out. From the first time I saw you, I loved you and knew that we would spend the rest of our lives together. So, it's only right that we make it "Official," and jump the broom soon as I come home. I spoke to the counselor and he approved my visiting list so pray that I will see you soon, my beautiful Queen.

Your Hubby,

"Roman"

TEN MINUTES TO ELEVEN THAT NIGHT,

Percy and Edmonds report to the front for work. Your ride's here," a C.O. announced over the intercom.

"You ready, fam," Bucky asked Roman as he approached Romans hut. "Yeah. Hell yeah. What's up wit' my jack, you gon' put it up"

"Nah, it's cool. Bring it wit'

After checking out at the message center. Bucky and Roman exited the building to a waiting facility vehicle,

"We right here, bro," Bucky told Roman.

"So, we out until six in the morn'," Roman asked.

"Yeah, we're on the out-count fo' tonight," Bucky said as they loaded into the car, Roman in the back and Bucky in the front.

"This ya friend," Ms. Flint asked.

"Yeah, dis my big homie," Bucky replied.

"Hmph, he's good-looking."

"Thanks," Roman said with a confused expression on his face, but what happened next really fucked him up.

"Mmmmuuu-ah," Bucky kissed Ms. Flint.

"Oh!" Was Roman's reaction.

"Ha ha ha ... What bro?! Dig my baby right here. She be holdin' ah nigga down. Don't you, bae?"

Our Love Is A Life Sentence

"That's all I know how to do. That's all I want to do," Ms. Flint replied.

"Mm mm mm," Roman expressed, shaking his head, and pointing a Bucky and then Ms. Flint.

"Ha ha ha," Ms. Flint laughed at Roman as she studied his facial expressions through the rearview mirror.

"We good fo' tonight, bae," Bucky asked Ms. Flint.

"Yes baby, we good. We just gotta switch cars," Ms. Flint replied. Five minutes later they hopped out of the white Malibu facility vehicle and got into a white Ford Explorer.

"Dig where we work, but we'll be back later," Bucky told Roman as he pointed to a huge industrial building.

"Just us," Roman asked.

"Yea-yup. We just make sure the AC and the heat or whatever don't break down on our shift."

"Dat's it?!" "Mainly. Yeah."

"Where we goin' now?"

"Ha ha ... Sit back, big bro. You'll see."

Our Love Is A Life Sentence

TWENTY MINUTES LATER, they pulled in to the parking lot of a Micro-Tel. "YOOO! What da...Ha ha," Roman said, closing his eyes, and shaking his head. He was completely fucked up about what he was seeing.

"Come on, bro," Bucky said as Ms. Flint shut down the SUV and threw her keys in her overnight bag. When they got out the car, Roman examined Ms. Flint's body and bit his fist watching her fat ass swish from side-to-side.

"Dat ass is fat, ain't it, big bro?" Bucky said when he looked back and seen Roman checking out the C.O.'s plumped ass. "Dat's all me. I got some'in' fo' you, tho. You got his key, bae," Bucky asked Ms. Flint.

"Yup. Here you go. Room 214," Ms. Flint said, digging into her overnight bag for Roman's hotel key-card, and handing it to him.

"There's some'in' nice up there fo' you, big bro," Bucky said with a smile spread across his face. "You got an hour, fam."

'Wight," Roman said, shaking his head up-and-down. He looked down at the key-card and headed for room 214.

"Ding!". The Elevator sounded. Roman stepped into the hallway and began to check the numbers on the door, "Might. Here we go," he said, slid the key-card downward in the door-slot. "Clickick!." The door unlocked and he twisted the door knob to open it.

316

"BAAAY-BEEE!!!" Diva screamed. Running into Roman's arms. "Yo, what's up, Dee?!!"

"Mmmmuuu-ah! Oh, ya ass is surprised, huh. Who you think was here? Ang' ain't tell you I was here, waitin' on ya ass. Hol' up ... Oh, you thought you was here to give my dick away, huh?!" Diva said, stepping back from a smiling Roman.

"Nah, I...

"Whatever! I should fuck you up" Diva said, playfully shoving Roman.

"Quit playin'. Come here," Roman said, wrapping his arms around Diva. Trying to kiss her but she turned her head.

"Give me ah kiss!" Roman said, trying to kiss a resisting Diva. Then she finally gave in, "Mmmmuuu-ah!"

"Come on, we only got like an hour, and shit. How long it takes you to get here," Roman asked.

"Almost four hours."

"It's crazy you traveled four hours just to be wit' me fo' an hour."

"I would've drove four hours fo' to just spend ah minute wit' you husband," Diva said with her arms wrapped around her man, and giving him a kiss.

"I mean you could stay here and come visit me tomorrow, and we can chill on ah visit. Shit's contact here."

"Yeah, I'll do dat," Diva said, wishing Roman would shut up and take her. It had been years since she had felt him inside of her. She told Roman that she would visit but she had no intentions of visiting him. She was there to free her man from his ten-year bid. While she was on the phone with the C.O. Ms. Flint making plans

to surprise him, the lawyer had called and told her that Roman would be released the following morning. Dice and his lady hustlers made plans of being there to pick their street god up, but Diva was keeping that information to herself for the time being.

Staring into Diva's eyes, Roman, finally took charge by passionately kissing Diva. As their tongues forcefully wrestled Diva's pussy soaked her lace panties, and Roman's dick grew a few inches.

"Oh baby, I missed you so much," Diva said in between kisses. "I missed you too," Roman said, scooping Diva off her feet, and carrying her to the bed.

Roman kick off his Tim's slipped his gray fleece over his head and stripped his green prison outfit from his lean, muscular body. Down to his wife-beater and brief's, Roman, help pull Diva's skin-tight jeans off. Putting her legs on his shoulders he began to kiss up her inner thigh. "Mmmmm-oooh," Diva moaned. The touch of his warm, wet lips gently pecking her soft flesh excited her. "Hiss hiss-hiss-hiss," she panted as she patiently waited for Roman's tongue to lick the pink slit of her pussy.

"Oh baby, I missed you. I've been wanting to taste dis pussy for so long," Seductively, Roman whispered. He pecked Diva's tight cunt through the red laced panties pressed closely to her snatch. "Hiss-hiss, eat it then. Taste it, baby. It's yours. Do what you wanna do to it," Diva said, pulling her panties to the right of her bald, swollen cunt-lips. "Smack-smack-slllssshh-lick-lick," sounded Roman's slippery, saliva-dripping oral-tentacle. Palming the back of Roman's head, Diva, thrust her pelvis, and fucked Roman's face, "Eat' it... Yes bae. .Yes, baby!" Pulling Roman's face from her pleasure hole, Diva framed it with her hands, and kissed him. His tongue taste sweet like her pussy. His face glistened from the pussy juices that covered him from his nose down.

"Lean back. Let me do you," Diva said, reaching to take Roman's dick in her. hand. Wetting her lips, she studied her man's thick prick that had a slight curve to it and began to lick the throbbing veins that ran up the sides of it.

"Like dat, slurp...Slllsssh," Diva asked Roman, looking him in his eyes.

"Fuck yes," Roman replied, faintly. Closing his eyes, he enjoyed the warmth of Diva's mouth suck the crown of his dick several times before deep-throating it. "Aaawwl, fuuuccck," Roman seductively whispered, opening his eyes to witness the beautiful creature devouring his beef stick. Slowly, Diva, stroked his dick up-and-down as her drool dripped down the sides of Roman's dick. Lubricating it just enough to make her mouth feel good and tight just like her pussy.

"Come here," Roman said, guiding Diva upward on to his body by her pretty face. Kissing him she reached under herself and positioned his cock to penetrate her hot, steamy, wet cunt. Kissing him more as her pussy slid down his pole, she sighed, "Uggghh... Ooh ... Ooh." As she took him in her thrust became more rhythmic, her pumps fierce and her pussy popped.

"HM, YEA! HM, YEA! HM, YEA ... LIKE DAT, BABY. LIKE DAT, BABY!" Roman repeated arousing gibberish as he met her pussy-popping with pussy-pounding, "YEA-YEA-YEA-YEA!" His hunk of meat showed Diva no mercy. Guiding her with both of his hands on her hips, Roman, talked shit as he lifted her and dropped her down on his throbbing slab of cum-maker, "CUM ON DAT DICK! CUM ON DAT DICK! CUM ON DAT DICK. Mmmmmm-oooohh...I'm bustin'...Bustin'..."

"Aaagggh-uggghh-oooohh ... Me too, daddy me too, daad-deee ... Mmmmm!"

They came at the same time as both of their bodies jerked uncontrollably.

Mmmuu-aack!

"Love you," Diva said, kissing Roman.

"Love you too," Roman replied.

FIVE THIRTY A.M., Bucky and Roman were being driven back to the Camp by Ms. Flint as more than a dozen men in navy blue windbreakers with guns surrounded the house of attorney Samuel Sholar.

BOOOM!!

"POLICE!!" Yelled the leading officer with yellow F.B.I letters screen-printed to the back of his jacket.

CRRAASSH!

"What the..." Samuel Sholar asked as his wife's PAPD coffee mug shattered. The Pennsylvania Police Department shield plastered to the side of the 'cup broke into pieces against the kitchen floor.

"WHAT IN THE HELL IS THIS ABOUT?!" Samuel asked.

"MALPRACTICE! You crooked, corrupt, ineffective motherfucker!" The leading officer yelled.

"Where's your search warrant?!"

"Right here. Read it and weep, motherfucker!"

"GOT IT! WE GOT IT!" Another F.B.I Officer came into the kitchen yelling, holding a big manila envelope up. It was the same manila envelope Diva had given Samuel. Inside was thirty thousand dollars of the fifty thousand dollars Diva had given to him.

"Fuck!" Samuel said under his breath. Seeing the envelope, he lowered the search warrant to his side. He suddenly knew what the raid and search was all about.

As the officer stacks of money onto the kitchen counter the leading officer pulled a personal note from his windbreaker jacket. "Yup, this is it," he said as he matched the serial numbers on the money to his note.

EIGHT FORTY-FIVE, "EDMONDS, REPORT TO THE CASE MANAGER'S OFFICE, REPORT TO THE CASE MANAGER'S OFFICE," an announcement came over the Camp's PA system.

"What the fuck he callin' me fo'?" Roman asked as him and Bucky sat in the Camp's TV Room discussing the night before.

"Shit, I 'on't know. It's only one way to find out. Get'cha ass up there and see ... ha ha ha."

"Ha ha ha, fuck you," Roman said, getting up to go to the case manager's office."

AT THE CASE MANAGER'S OFFICE, come in, Mr. Edmonds," the case manager motioned after seeing Roman about to knock on his office door.

"How you doin'?" Roman asked, nervously.

"Im okay. You?" The case manager asked, looking over a release document faxed to him by the courts.

"I'm a'ight."

"Well, this should make your day a lot better," the case manager said, tapping on the document's laying on his desk, "Mr. Edmonds you're being immediately released. You need to 'collect all your things and report back up here for processing. You need to be off federal grounds within the hour."

BACK IN THE UNIT, Roman went to the TV Room to get Bucky, "Bro, look here," Roman said to Bucky.

"What up, fam. What they talkin' bout?" Bucky said, talking to Roman outside of the TV Room.

"I'm outta dis bitch, lil bro!"

"Big Homie, fo' real?!"

"Yeah. I ain't wanna say shit 'til shit was final, but I'm out. They are giving me an Immediate Release. My lawyer was on some corrupt shit as far as my case so they cuttin' me loose."

"Daaamn. Well, let me get'cha info an' shit."

"No doubt. You know I gotta keep in touch wit' you. You outta here next year tho, right?"

"Yeah... yup."

"Then you know we gon' hook up. All the shit you did fo' me. You know I got you!"

"Dat's what's up," Bucky said as him and Roman shook hands, and embraced.

AT BLONDE'S HOUSE, Dice could see her reaching for her .380 caliber Browning semi-automatic pistol in the reflection of her screen door. As he was walking out of the front door. Quickly drawing his Colt .45 out of reflex, Dice, turned and let off a shot.

PLOW!

As did Blonde

BURR-LACK!"

CRRAAASSHH!

Sounded the screen door glass behind Dice. Their gunshots and the sound of glass shattering echoed off the apartment walls and mimicked thunder, hit once, Blonde uttered a shrill yelp, "Oof," and collapsed. Suddenly her body fell and bounced off the wood-panel floor. The fall made her gun slide approximately four feet from her opened right hand and stop with the barrel aimed towards her,

Seeing Blonde laying motion less made Dice panic beyond reason. He paused as his heart paced at a high rapid speed, adrenaline flowed through his veins, and he gasped with deep, short breathes as his mind instantly replayed what happened only seconds before:

'Wight, I'll hit you in ah minute," he said to Blonde, opening her front door. Through the screen door glass, he seen Blonde going for her strap. He drew his weapon and fired once

PLOW!!!

As he squeezed off his shot, he shifted his body sideways on some Matrix-type shit. Which allowed him to avoid the shot that shattered the screen door.

CRRAAASSHH!

Simultaneously, Blonde, was blown back off her, feet.

Bloomp-Oomp-Oomp-Oomp!

Was the reverberating sound of Blonde's body dropping and bouncing off the glossy-wood floor.

Dice's single-shot inwardly ruptured Blonde's flesh and skull. Blood streamed down her face from the cracked wound in her forehead. The shock of being shot and dying- pried her eyes wide-open. Within a matter of seconds, her body became lifeless and she slipped from lives dominion to death. Staring aimlessly into the spinning ceiling fan it was as if she was searching for her lost soul somewhere up there in the abyss of darkness that fell over her being.

Dice ran over to the lady-hustler that he had grown to love, and hovered over her body before his rubbery-legs crumbled him to the floor. Tilting his head back, he murmured several senseless obscenities mixed with regret, and braced the sides of his temples with both hands; his left hand balled into a fist and the other still clutched the murder-weapon.

Studying Blonde's grim-faced, tears wailed and drew beads of pain that poured from the rims of his blood-shot peepers as she looked past him with a dead stare. With tears running down the cheeks of his face he tried to yell out, but at first, his search for inner strength to shriek outwardly drew a silent cry. Then Roman's number two man wailed loudly, "Wh-Wh-Why?! Why, Blonde, WHHHYYYYY?!"

"Dice ... Dice...Bay-be! DICE?!" Blonde called out, waking Dice from his dream. He had drove the entire four hours up to the jail to pick up Roman. Waiting for him to exit the Camp he had fell asleep.

"You know you can't leave no loose ends ... I 'on't want you facin' ah life sentence," Was the words he heard Roman saying before he passed out.

"Is dat him?' Blonde asked.

"Yeah, dat's my nigga!"

"Huss-baaannd!" They heard Diva yell as she jumped out of her rental and ran, up to Roman as he exited the Camp's entrance.

"SNAP-SNAP!"

Dice and his girls got out of his SUV and walked up to Roman.

SNAP-SNAP-SNAP-SNAP!

"What up, bro. Good to see you on the other side of dem gates," Dice said, embracing his best friend.

SNAP-SNAP-SNAP!

"Baby, dis is Blonde..."

"Hey," Roman said, embracing Blonde.

"...And dis is 'Vette," Diva said, introducing Blonde and Evette to Roman.

"SNAP-SNAP-SNAP-SNAP!"

"Heard a lot about y'all. Thanks, fo' holdin' it down fo' me while I was gon'. I'm back now, tho. Y'all ready to get dis paper out here?"

SNAP-SNAP!

"Hell yeah..."

"You know it," Blonde and Evette responded.

"Well, let's get it!" Roman said, wrapping his arm around Diva as they walked to their vehicles. What neither of them knew was they were under surveillance. DEA Agent's had captured Roman's release taking snap-shots from an undercover car parked thirty-feet away from them. In total, they had taken fifteen pictures and would follow them back to Pittsburgh where they would continue their surveillance. Until they could build a solid case against the small group of gangsters that had conspired against and beat the government.

THE END.

ABOUT THE AUTHOR

Our Love Is A Life Sentence

MORE BOOKS BY THIS AUTHOR

IF YOU ENJOYED THIS BOOK PLEASE LEAVE A REVIEW

Made in the USA
Middletown, DE
01 October 2024